# GEORGIA COUNTY COURTHOUSES

## THE ARCHITECTURE OF LIVING MONUMENTS

### RHETT TURNER

Library of Congress Control Number: 2013951207
International Standard Book Number: 978-0-88240-996-2

Photographer: Rhett Turner
Designer: Jennifer Markson, The Euclid Shop
Copy Editor: Susan Lauzau
Production Manager: Karen Matsu Greenberg

Published by Graphic Arts Books
An imprint of

GRAPHIC ARTS
BOOKS®

P.O. Box 56118
Portland, Oregon 97238-6118
503-254-5591
www.graphicartsbooks.com

Ptinted in China

1  3  5  7  9  10  8  6  4  2

# ACKNOWLEDGEMENTS

Putting a book together for publishing is definitely a team effort. It starts, of course, with a concept, a fierce commitment to that concept, and an aligning of forces with experts who can help execute the plan. I would like to thank Chris Boot from Aperture Foundation, who looked at the portfolio of Georgia Courthouse photographs and liked them, giving me the confidence to move forward. He suggested meeting Michael Friedman who in turn introduced me to Jeffrey Batzli and Jennifer Markson, who designed the book. Without their help the book would not have been finished. I also want to thank my wife, Angela Della Costanza Turner, for putting up with my grandiose ideas and for providing the space that allowed me to fulfill my travel plans and chronicle every county in the state of Georgia. My partner at Red Sky Productions, Greg Pope, provided continued encouragement to stay on task, and I'm so grateful. Robert Glenn Ketchum, a great friend and photographer, who I had the privilege to intern with in Alaska many years, ago, has been inspiring me for many years and his influence continues to resonate. And, finally, I would like to thank Iago Corazza, who has helped me polish my craft as a still photographer during our insightful travels to many corners of the globe.

# THE ARCHITECTURE OF GEORGIA COURTHOUSES

As a documentary filmmaker, I have the opportunity to make films on subjects I'm passionate about. My two most recent productions have been *Chattahoochee: From Water War to Water Vision* and *Chattahoochee Unplugged.* The first—*Chattahoochee: From Water War to Water Vision*—was about the twenty-year struggle over water rights in Alabama, Georgia, and Florida. The second is *Chattahoochee Unplugged,* which documents the removal of two dams in Columbus, Georgia, a project that restored the Coweta Falls to its former glory and installed a world-class white water course.

I also am a still photographer who has traveled the world taking photographs in countries including Libya, Ethiopia, Sudan, Yemen, Burkina Faso, Togo, Benin, Myanmar, and Laos. When not globetrotting, I've made my home and workbase in Atlanta, but I still didn't really know my roots. In 2006, I was hired by the Georgia Department of Economic Development to produce a video that state officials could use to show international companies what a beautiful and business-friendly state Georgia is. While traveling around the state shooting this video, I saw several Georgia courthouses and was amazed by their architecture. From that experience came the idea to make a photography book on Georgia's courthouses. It took me until 2012 to travel around my state to all 159 county seats, to photograph every county courthouse in Georgia. In the process, I changed my attitude about Georgia, because I am also a history buff, and I watch the History Channel in my spare time. I fell in love with the Georgia countryside and with the state's history.

Among the history highlights for me was this fact: the first state flag of Texas was designed by Joanna Troutman, who gave a Lone Star Flag to Georgia soldiers on their way to fight for the independence of the State of Texas. The emblem was incorporated into the current flag of Texas. Another, interesting piece of history concerns General Longstreet of the Confederacy; he spent his life in Gainesville, Georgia, in Hall County, after the American Civil War. Dade County in northwest Georgia is famous for being the first county to secede from the Union during the Civil War, and it didn't return to the Union until July 4, 1945. It was known as the State of Dade. I find this history fascinating, and it is all to be found at our county seats throughout the state. The courthouse buildings themselves are likewise remarkable examples of public architecture—and that is why I traveled to all 159 counties of Georgia to document these centers of law and communities in the small towns of Georgia.

*—Rhett Turner*

# GEORGIA
## COUNTY COURTHOUSES

APPLING COUNTY 1907-08

*Opposite*

ATKINSON COUNTY 1920

*Above*

BALDWIN COUNTY COURTHOUSE

**BALDWIN COUNTY 1995-97**

**BACON COUNTY 1919**

**BAKER COUNTY 1906**

# BANKS COUNTY 1863

BANKS COUNTY WAS CREATED BY ACT OF DEC. 11, 1858 from Franklin and Habersham Counties. It was named for Dr. Richard Banks (1784-1850), whose reputation as physician and surgeon extended over north Ga. and S.C. Especially noted for treating Indians for smallpox, he practiced medicine in Gainesville from 1832 until his death. First officers of Banks County, commissioned March 19, 1859, were: William P. Richards, Sheriff; James Anderson, Clk. Sup. Ct.; William H. Means, Clk. Inf. Ct.; Archibald McDonald, Coroner; Pierce C. Key, Surveyor; Fountain G. Moss, Ord.; Thomas Ausburn, Tax Col.; Elijah Owens. Tax Rec.

# BARROW COUNTY 1920

BARROW COUNTY WAS CREATED BY ACT OF JULY 7, 1914 from Gwinnett, Jackson and Walton Counties. It was named for David Crenshaw Barrow, Chancellor of the University of Georgia for many years. Born in Oglethorpe County, October 18, 1852, he died in Athens, January 11, 1929. Affectionately known to thousands as "Uncle Dave," he spent most of his life teaching. First officers of Barrow County, commissioned January 11, 1915, were: H.G. Hill, Ordinary; Geo. N. Bagwell, Clk. Sup. Ct.; H. O. Camp, Sheriff; J. A. Still, Tax Receiver; Alonzo N. Williams, Tax Collector; J. W. Nowell, Treasurer; R. L. Griffith, Surveyor; Tom McElhannon, Coroner; W. M. Holsenbeck, Co. School Supt.

# Bartow County 1902

Originally Cass, Bartow County was created by Act of Dec. 3, 1832 from Cherokee County. The name was changed Dec. 6, 1861 to honor Gen. Francis S. Bartow (1816-1861). Confederate political leader and soldier, who fell mortally wounded at the First Battle of Manassas, while leading the 7th and 8th Ga. Vols. of his brigade. His last words were said to be, "They have killed me, boys, but never give up." First officers of this county, commissioned March 9, 1833, were: Benjamin F. Adair, Sheriff; Chester Hawks, Clerk Superior Court; Leathern Rankin, Clerk Inferior Court; Nealy Goodwin, Surveyor; John Pack, Coroner.

## Ben Hill County 1909

Ben Hill County, created by Act of July 31, 1906 from Irwin and Wilcox Counties, was named for Benjamin Harvey Hill (1823-1882), "one of America's greatest orators." A staunch supporter of the administration in the Confederate Senate, after the War Between the States he was an influential member of the U. S. House of Representatives and Senate. First officers of Ben Hill County, commissioned Jan. 5, 1907, were: C. M. Wise, Ordinary; D. W. M. Whitley, Clerk Superior Court; W. H. Fountain, Sheriff; E. Gibbs, Tax Receiver; W. L. Smith, Tax Collector, J. H. Goodman, Treasurer; Oscar Barron, Surveyor; William McCormick, Coroner.

# BERRIEN COUNTY 1899

BERRIEN COUNTY, CREATED BY ACT OF FEB. 25, 1856, was named for John MacPherson Berrien, "the American Cicero," who was born Aug. 23, 1781 and died Jan. 1, 1856. He was Judge of the Eastern Circuit, U. S. Senator and U. S. Attorney General. The county seat, Nashville was named for Gen. Francis Nash of N. C., distinguished soldier of the Revolution. First county officers, commissioned April 21, 1856, were: Sher., John Studstill; Clk. of Courts, Richard A. Peeples; Tax Rec., John A. Money; Tax Col., John M. Futch; Cor., James Dobson; Sur., Seaborn J. Bradford; Ord., John Lindsey.

# BIBB COUNTY 1924

BIBB COUNTY WAS CREATED BY ACT OF DEC. 9, 1822 from Houston, Jones, Monroe and Twiggs Counties. It was named for Dr. William Wyatt Bibb (1781-1820) of Elbert County. Dr. Bibb, physician, legislator, Congressman, Senator, was appointed Governor of the Territory of Alabama by Pres. Madison and was the first elective Governor of the State of Alabama. First officers of Bibb County, commissioned Feb. 12, 1823, were: Nicholas W. Wells, Clerk of Superior Court; James Flewellen, Clerk of Inferior Court; John B. Grace, Surveyor. Isaac Philips was made Surveyor July 16, 1823, Jonathan H. Hudson was commissioned Sheriff, Jan. 9, 1824.

# BLECKLEY COUNTY 1914

THIS COUNTY, CREATED BY AN ACT OF THE GEORGIA Legislature July 30, 1912, is named for Chief Justice Logan E. Bleckley, of the Georgia Supreme Court, one of the greatest jurists in the history of this State. Born in Rabun County in 1827, he served as a Confederate soldier, resumed his law practice after the war, was an Associate Justice of the Supreme Court 1875-1880 and Chief Justice 1887-1894. Among the first Bleckley County officers were Sheriff J.A. Floyd, Superior Court Clerk J. T. Deese, Ordinary W. M. Wynne, Tax Receiver Jim Holland, Tax Collector W. D. Porter, Treasurer J. R. Taylor, Coroner Morgan Barrs, Surveyor W. H. Berryhill, Comm. Of Roads and Revenue J. B. Hinson.

BRANTLEY COUNTY 1930

**BROOKS COUNTY 1859-64**

*Opposite left*

**BRYAN COUNTY 1938**

*Above*

# BULLOCH COUNTY 1894

BULLOCH COUNTY WAS CREATED BY ACT OF FEB. 8, 1796 from Bryan and Screven Counties. Originally, it contained parts of Evans, Candler, Emanuel and Jenkins Counties. It was named for Archibald Bulloch (1730-1777), Revolutionary leader, elected Pres. of the Executive Council of Georgia, Jan. 20, 1776. He was first Provisional Governor of Georgia, Jan. 22, 1776 until his death, Feb. 22, 1777. First County Officers, commissioned March 25, 1796, were: Charles McCall, Jr. Sheriff; Andrew E. Wells, Clerk Sup. Ct.; George Elliott, Clerk Inf. Ct.; Francis Wells, Register of Probate; James Bird, Surveyor; Garrott Williams Coroner.

## BUTTS COUNTY 1898

## BURKE COUNTY 1857

THIS COUNTY, CREATED BY ACT OF THE LEGISLATURE December 24, 1825, is named for Capt. Sam Butts killed in the Indian War of 1814 at the Battle of Chalibbee. At Indian Springs, now a State Park, were signed the Treaties with the Creeks giving Georgia respectively all lands between the Flint and Ocmulgee Rivers north to the Chattahoochee, and all the remaining Indian lands in the state. Among the first County Officers were: Sheriff Isaac Nolen, Clerk of Superior Court Abel L. Robinson, Clerk of Inferior Court Thomas Thornton, Coroner Wm. B. Smith and Surveyor Willie Terrell.

## CALHOUN COUNTY 1930-35

This county, created by Act of the Legislature Feb. 20, 1854, is named for John C. Calhoun, famed South Carolina Statesman, who resigned as Vice President of the United States in 1832 to return to the U. S. Senate and defend States Rights in debates with Daniel Webster. He served as Secretary of War (1817-25) and Secretary of State (1844-45).

First Calhoun County Officers were: Sheriff Wm. H. Pierce, Clerk Joseph W. Roberts, Ordinary Wm. S. Harris, Tax Receiver H. W. Wilkins, Tax Collector Kinion Strickland, Surveyor Charles Stewart and Coroner Amos Forehand.

## CAMDEN COUNTY 1928

## CARROLL COUNTY 1928

CARROLL COUNTY, CREATED BY AN ACT OF THE GEORGIA LEGISLATURE IN DECEMBER, 1826, proudly bears the name of Charles Carroll, of Carrollton.

Charles Carroll was born in Annapolis, Maryland, in 1737. He attended preparatory schools in this country but completed his education in France and England. At the age of 28 he returned home to settle down and his father gave him a large estate near Frederick, Md. known as Carrollton Manor. From then on he became known as "Charles Carroll of Carrollton." Although extremely wealthy and risking the loss of all his property, Charles Carroll boldly threw himself into Revolutionary activities. He served in the Continental Congress in 1776-78, and soon after his election was appointed by the Congress along with Benjamin Franklin and Samuel Chase to unsuccessfully seek Canadian support for the Continental cause. He became one of Maryland's first United States Senators serving from 1789 through 1792.

Charles Carroll played an important part in early railroad and canal building in the United Sates and laid the cornerstone of the Baltimore & Ohio Railroad in 1828, at the age of ninety-one. Four years later he died, the last survivor of the 56 signers of the Declaration of Independence.

## CANDLER COUNTY 1921

CANDLER COUNTY WAS CREATED BY AN ACT OF THE GEORGIA LEGISLATURE JULY 17, 1914, out of portions of Bulloch, Emanuel and Tattnall Counties, and named for Gov. Allen D. Candler (1834-1910). Gov. Candler is famed for the preservation of Colonial and Confederate records and being the first compiler of State records. Among the first officers of Candler County were Ordinary George R. Trapnell, Sheriff Charles M. Harper, Superior Court Clerk Joshua Everett, Tax Receiver O. L. Patterson, Tax Collector G. B. Hendricks, Surveyor J. D. McLean, Coroner T. D. Joiner and Treasurer Morgan Holloway.

# CATOOSA COUNTY 1939

CREATED DECEMBER 5, 1853, THE COUNTY HAS AN Indian name, Ringgold bears the name of Major Samuel Ringgold, who died of wounds received at the Mexican War battle of Palo Alto in 1846. Taylor's Ridge, visible for miles, is named for the Indian chief Richard Taylor. Catoosa Springs, four miles to the east, and Gordon Springs, ten miles south, were colorful ante-bellum summer resorts. The bloody Chickamauga battle was fought seven miles to the west, the battlefield now being a National Military Park.

## CHARLTON COUNTY 1928

CREATED BY AN ACT OF FEBRUARY 18, 1854 OUT OF CAMDEN County, Charlton County was named for Judge Robert M. Charlton of Savannah. Trader's Hill (Fort Alert), an important shipping point and head of navigation on St. Mary's River, was the first County Site. In 1901, Folkston became the County Site, after the Savannah, Florida & Western RR was in operation. The first County Officers, elected in April 1854, were: Daniel R. Dedge, Sheriff; J. H. Oliver, Clerk of both Courts; Francis M. Smith, Ordinary; John E. Gibson, Tax Receiver; J. H. Bessant, Surveyor; James S. Bennett, Coroner; Louis N. G. Strickland, soon replaced by H. Roddenberry, Tax Collector.

## Chatham County 1978

## Chattahoochee County 1975-76

CHATTAHOOCHEE COUNTY, CREATED BY ACT OF FEBRUARY 13, 1854, was cut off from Muscogee and Marion Counties. It was named for the Chattahoochee River. Its courthouse, constructed in 1854, was built of select heart lumber from the Long Leaf Pine by slave labor. First county officers, commissioned March 11, 1854, were: William W. Bussey, Sheriff; N. N. Howard, Clerk of Superior Court; Ezekiel Walters, Clerk Inferior Court; Abner Smith, Ordinary; William H. Askew, Tax Receiver; Stephen Parker, Tax Collector; Littleton Morgan, Surveyor; William S. Howard, Coroner.

# CHATTOOGA COUNTY 1909

CHATTOOGA COUNTY WAS CREATED BY ACT OF DEC. 28, 1838 from Floyd and Walker Counties. It was named for the river which flows through the county; called Chattooga by the Cherokee Indians. Sequoyah (George Guess or Gist), inventor of the Cherokee Alphabet, was born and lived for some time near Alpine in Chattooga County. First County Officers, commissioned February 5, 1839, were G. T. Hopkins, Clerk Superior Court; I. N. Bibb, Clerk Inferior Court; W. T. Kellet, Sheriff; I. McNeally, Coroner.

# CHEROKEE COUNTY 1928-29

CREATED DECEMBER 3, 1832 FROM CHEROKEE INDIAN lands, and named in memory of the Cherokees. Early settlers tried to start silk production, but were not successful, and today there remains no trace of this except Canton, hopefully named for the Chinese silk center.

The Marietta and North Georgia Railroad reached Canton in 1879, providing a considerable stimulus to development.

The locally financed and managed textile mill, which began operations in 1900, had provided a payroll of much local importance.

## CLARKE COUNTY 1914

CLARKE COUNTY, CREATED BY ACT OF DEC. 5, 1801 FROM Jackson County, originally contained Oconee and parts of Madison and Green Counties. It was named for Gen. Elijah Clarke who came to Wilkes County, Ga., from N. C. in 1774 and fought through Ga. and S. C. during the Revolutionary War. He engaged in several battles with the Indians and signed treaties with the Cherokees in 1783 and Creeks in 1783 and 1785. He died Dec. 15, 1799. First Officers of Clarke County, commissioned Dec. 31, 1801, were: Abner Bankston, Sheriff; Bedford Brown, Clk. Sup. Ct.; Gabriel Hubert, Clk. Inf. Ct; Stephen Nobles, Surveyor; Daniel Conner, Coroner.

# CLAY COUNTY 1871-73

THIS COUNTY CREATED BY ACT OF THE LEGISLATURE Feb. 16, 1854, is named for Henry Clay, famous statesman who died in 1852. Near Fort Gaines, the County Site, stood the actual Fort built in 1816 for defense in the Creek Indian Wars and named for Gen. Edmond P. Gaines who ordered its construction. Among the first County Officers were: Sheriff George R. Holloway, Clerk of the Superior & Inferior Courts Warren Sutton, Ordinary John H. Jones, Tax Receiver John H. Gilbert, Tax Collector Peter Lee, County Surveyor Bennett H. Thornton and Coroner Churchill Patrick.

# Clayton County 1898

Clayton County was created by Act of Nov. 30, 1858 from Fayette and Henry Counties. It was named for Augustine Smith Clayton, born at Fredericksburg, Va., Nov. 27, 1783, who moved to Georgia before 1800. A graduate of the U. of Ga., he was a lawyer, legislator, judge. During two terms in Congress he opposed tariff and U. S. bank measures. He died in Athens, June 21, 1839. First officers of Clayton County, commissioned Jan. 13, 1859, were: Robert K. Holliday, Clk. Sup. Ct.; A. J. Hayes, Clk. Inf. Ct.; James McConnell, Ord; William Gunter, Tax Rec.; Jefferson Kirkland, Tax Col.; B. W. Bonner, Surveyor; John K. Landers, Coroner; J. H. Waldrop, Sheriff.

CLINCH COUNTY 1896

## COBB COUNTY 1965-66

CREATED DECEMBER 3, 1832, AND NAMED FOR JUDGE THOMAS W. COBB, A former U. S. Senator. Marietta was named for his wife. Fertile lands gave impetus to farming; ample water power encouraged industries. People from further south sought Marietta as a summer resort due to delightful climate and society. Cobb County sacrificed much for the Southern Confederacy; ravaged by war, it fought slowly upward through reconstruction. In recent years industry has brought wealth and growth to the area.

## COFFEE COUNTY 1940

THIS COUNTY, CREATED BY ACT OF THE LEGISLATURE FEBRUARY 9, 1854, IS NAMED FOR Gen. John Coffee who served in the Indian Wars and was a Member of Congress in 1833-36. He built the "Old Coffee Road," which forms part of the border between Berrien and Coffee Counties, over which to transport troops and supplies to Florida. Among the first County Officers were: Sheriff B. H. Tanner, Ordinary Thomas Mobley, Clerk of Superior and Inferior Courts Whittington Moore, Tax Receiver John W. Machet, Tax Collector James R. Smith, Coroner Sim Parker and Surveyor Carver.

# COLQUITT COUNTY 1902

This County, created by Act of the Legislature February 25, 1856, is named for Hon. Walter T. Colquitt who had recently died. A famous lawyer and Methodist preacher, he served in Congress in 1839-40 and 1842-43, and in the Senate from 1843 to '48. "As an advocate Judge Colquitt stood alone in Georgia." Among the first County Officers were: Sheriff Jacob F. Reichert, Clerk of Superior Court William McLeod, Ordinary Hardy Chastain, Tax Receiver John A. Alderman, Tax Collector Job Turner, Coroner Elijah Tillman and Surveyor Amos Turner.

COOK COUNTY 1938-39

*Opposite*

COLUMBIA COUNTY 1856

*Above*

# COOK COUNTY

This County, created by Act of the Legislature July 30, 1918, is named for Gen. Philip Cook who fought in the States and Seminole Wars. He served in Congress from 1872 to '82. Secretary of State for Georgia 1890-94 and 1898-1918. He served as one of the Commissioners to erect the present State Capitol. Among the first County Officers were: Sheriff W. T. Dougherty, Ordinary C.O. Smith, Clerk of Superior Court F.R. Booth, Tax Receiver J.A. Kinnard, Tax Collector J.B. Wright, Treasurer W.M. Tyson, Surveyor E.R. Slade and Coroner A.D. Wiseman.

GEORGIA HISTORICAL COMMISSION

037-1

SN

COOK COUNTY COURT HOUSE

COWETA, AN ORIGINAL COUNTY, WAS CREATED BY ACTS OF June 9, 1825 and Dec. 11, 1826 from Creek cessions of Jan. 24, 1826 and Mar. 31, 1826. It was named Coweta to perpetuate the fame of the head chief of the Coweta Towns, Gen. William McIntosh, half-blood Creek Indian. Gen. McIntosh, daring soldier and useful ally during the War with the British, was killed in his home by some of his own people after he signed the Treaty at Indian Springs, ceding land to the Whites. First officers of Coweta County, commissioned May 15, 1827 were: Josiah B. Beall, Sheriff; John F. Beavers, Clk. Sup. Ct.; Henry Taulett, Clk. Inf. Ct.; Irwin Baggett, Surveyor; Shadrach Green, Coroner.

## COWETA COUNTY 1904

## CRISP COUNTY 1950

## CRAWFORD COUNTY 1832

THIS COUNTY CREATED BY ACTS OF THE LEGISLATURE Dec. 9 & 23, 1822, is named for William H. Crawford, Georgia statesman who was Secretary of the Treasury at the time the County was established. At the County Site, Knoxville, lived Joanna E. Troutman (Mrs. Vinson) who is credited with designing the Lone Star Flag of the Republic of Texas. When a company of Macon Volunteers under Col. William A. Ward marched through on the way to Texas Miss Troutman presented them with a white silk flag bearing a single, large blue star, which she had designed and made.

CRISP COUNTY WAS CREATED BY ACT OF AUG 17, 1905 FROM the House of Representatives, 1891-1893. First officers of Dooly County. It was named for Charles Frederick Crisp County, commissioned October 10, 1905, were: Crisp (1845-1896), Georgia lawyer, judge, Congressman, S. W. Coney, Ordinary; J. A. Littlejohn, Clk. Sup. Ct.; who was born in Sheffield, England, of actor parents G. W. Sheppard, Sheriff; J. M. Davis, Tax Rec.; John touring the British Isles. Judge Crisp served as Speaker of Cheeves, Surveyor; L. M. Sumner, Coroner.

## DADE COUNTY 1926

OFTEN CALLED THE "STATE OF DADE," BECAUSE AS LEGEND has it, the county seceded from the Union ahead of Georgia, and only returned to the Union July 4, 1945. Created December 25, 1837, and named for Major Francis Langhorne Dade, killed by Indians in Florida, December, 1835. The county seat was first named Salem, then changed to Trenton in 1840.

Outstanding picturesque mountain scenery accounts for the creation of Cloudland State Park. Rich coal and iron deposits have been worked since Ante-Bellum times.

## DAWSON COUNTY 1858

## DECATUR COUNTY 1902

DECATUR COUNTY WAS CREATED BY ACT OF DEC. 8, 1823 from Early County. Sessions were cut off later to form part of Seminole and Grady Counties. It was named for Stephen Decatur (1779-1820), naval officer who served with great gallantry at Tripoli and in the War of 1812. In 1815, he commanded the expedition against the Dey of Algiers, forcing the Dey to renounce claims to tribute from the U. S. First County Officers, commissioned May 5, 1824 were: John H. Gray, Sheriff; Jacob Harrell, Coroner; R. B. Douglass, Surveyor; Daniel O'Neel, Clerk Superior Court. Daniel O'Neel was commissioned Clerk of Inferior Court, also, on June 11, 1824.

DeKalb County 1916

DODGE COUNTY 1908

# DOOLY COUNTY

DOOLY COUNTY 1890-92

THIS COUNTY, CREATED BY ACTS OF THE LEGISLATURE MAY 15 & Dec. 24, 1821, is named for Col. John Dooly of Revolutionary fame who was murdered in his home by Tories in 1780. The original County Site was at Berrien on the Flint River in 1823, the name being changed to Drayton in 1833. In the early '40's the Legislature voted to move the Site to another town named Berrien but this was not done. In the late '40's the Site was moved to Vienna which is famed as the home of "elder statesman" Walter F. George, U. S. Senator for more than thirty years, elected in 1922.

## DOUGLAS COUNTY 1957

THIS COUNTY, CREATED BY ACT OF THE LEGISLATURE OCTOBER 17, 1870, IS NAMED for Stephen A. Douglas, the "Little Giant," a Vermonter who was Congressman from Illinois 1843 to '47, Senator from '47 to '61, and Democratic candidate for President in 1860 on the ticket with Gov. Herschel V. Johnson, of Georgia, for Vice President. Among the first County Officers were: Sheriff T. H. Sellman, Clerk of Superior Court A. L. Gorman, Ordinary Wm. Hindman, Tax Receiver Jno. M. James, Tax Collector M. D. Watkins, Treasurer C. P. Bower, Coroner S. W. Biggers and Surveyor John M. Hughey.

## DOUGHERTY COUNTY 1968

THIS COUNTY, CREATED BY ACT OF THE LEGISLATURE DECEMBER 15, 1853, IS NAMED for Charles Dougherty of Athens, noted ante-bellum lawyer and jurist and strong advocate of states rights. In the Creek War in 1836 the Indians were driven out at the Battle of Chickasawhachee Swamp. Among the first County Officers were: Sheriff John H. Phillips, Ordinary William E. Smith, Clerk of Superior Court Samuel D. Irvin, Clerk of Inferior Court Thos. J. Johnston, Tax Receiver Bennett Adams, Tax Collector Redding O. Rutland, Coroner Sherrod Hook and Surveyor Thos. G. Westfall.

## Early County 1904-05

## Echols County 1956

THIS COUNTY, CREATED BY ACT OF THE Legislature Dec. 13, 1858, is named for Col. Robert M. Echols, for 24 years a member of the General Assembly; He was a President of the Georgia Senate and a Brigadier General in the Mexican War during which he died. Among the first County Officers were: Sheriff James S. Carter, Ordinary James P. Y. Higdon, Clerk of Superior & Inferior Courts Jesse P. Prescott, Tax Receiver John E. McMullen, Tax Collector Samuel E. Prescott, Treasurer James Carter, Surveyor Duncan McLeod and Coroner John Sellers.

## EFFINGHAM COUNTY 1908

*Opposite*

## ELBERT COUNTY 1893-94

*Above*

EMANUEL COUNTY 2002

This County, created by Act of the Legislature Aug. 11, 1914, is named for Gen. Clement A. Evans, soldier, lawyer, minister, statesman, & author, who died in 1911. He commanded Gordon's old division in the last charge of the Army of Northern Virginia and surrendered under Lee at Appomattox "with guns still hot from firing until the last hour." Among the first County Officers were: Sheriff T. W. Rogers, Ordinary W. H. Brewton, Clerk of Superior Court T. R. Tippins, Tax Receiver A. V. Smith, Tax Collector Daniel Sikes, Treasurer James S. Hogan and Surveyor A. D. Eason.

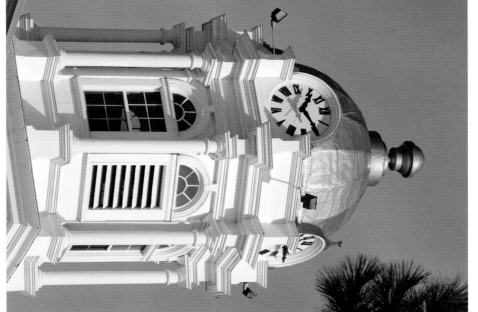

## Evans County 1923

FANNIN COUNTY 1937

# FAYETTE COUNTY 1825

THIS COUNTY, CREATED BY ACTS OF THE LEGISLATURE MAY 15 AND DECEMBER 24, 1821, IS named for the Marquis de LaFayette, famous French General who came to this country to fight under General George Washington in the Revolutionary War. After returning to France he revisited Georgia in 1825. Fayetteville was incorporated and made the County Site in 1823. Among the first County Officers were: Sheriff John Welch, Clerk of Superior Court Thomas A. Dobbs, Clerk of Inferior Court Jonathan Dobbs, Coroner John Calhoun and Surveyor James Adams.

## FLOYD COUNTY 1892-93

FLOYD COUNTY WAS CREATED BY ACT OF DEC. 3, 1832 out of Cherokee County. Originally, it included parts of Chattooga, Polk and Gordon Counties. Early settlers cam from Tenn., S. C., and older parts of Ga. The county was named for Maj. Gen. John Floyd (1794-1829), Legislator, Congressman, Gen. of Ga. Militia, Commander of Ga. troops against the Creeks in 1813 and Commander of troops at Savannah. First officers of Floyd County, commissioned March 18, 1833, were: Andrew H. Johnston, Sheriff; Edwin G. Rogers, Clerk Superior Court; Philip W. Hemphill, Clerk Inferior Court; John Smithwicke, Surveyor; Lemuel Milligan, Coroner.

FORSYTH COUNTY 1977

Franklin County 1906

# FULTON COUNTY 1911-14

FULTON COUNTY WAS CREATED OUT OF DEKALB County by an Act of the Legislature approved December 20, 1853 (as amended and corrected by the Act of February 7, 1854). The City of Atlanta was made the County Seat. From 1872 until 1932, parts of Milton and Campbell Counties were added to Fulton. In 1932 complete consolidation with Milton and Campbell Counties and the annexation from Cobb of the Town of Roswell fixed the boundaries of the County.

The first officers of the original County, commissioned February 15, 1854, were as follows: Jonas S. Smith, Sheriff; Benjamin F. Bomar, Clerk, Superior Court; Columbus M. Payne, Clerk, Inferior Court; Joseph H. Mead, Ordinary; Madison S. Yoakum, Tax Receiver; John M. Smith, Tax Collector; James Bartlett, Surveyor; John K. Landers, Coroner.

The legislative act creating Fulton County did not specify whom the name honored. The names of two persons have been suggested: Robert Fulton, inventor of the steamboat *Clermont*, and Hamilton Fulton, Chief Engineer of the State in 1826. In 1954 the Fulton County Centennial Commission, based on research by several Atlanta historians, gave that honor to Robert Fulton.

GILMER COUNTY 1898, 1934

# GLASCOCK COUNTY 1919

THIS COUNTY, CREATED BY ACT OF THE Legislature Dec. 19, 1857, is named for Gen. Thomas Glascock who served in the War of 1812 and the Seminole War. He was a Speaker of the Georgia House of Representatives and a Member of Congress from 1835 to '39. Among the first County Officers were: Sheriff Augustus C. Reece, Ordinary Francis M. Kelly, Clerk of Superior Court Richard Walden, Clerk of Inferior Court Daniel Glover, Tax Receiver Abraham Brassell, Tax Collector Tobias Logue, Surveyor Seaborn Kitchens and Coroner Seaborn Glover.

# GLYNN COUNTY 1907

GLYNN COUNTY, ONE OF THE EIGHT ORIGINAL Counties of Georgia, was organized under the 1777 Constitution of the State of Georgia. It was named in honor of John Glynn, a member of the British House of Commons who defended the cause of the American Colonies in the difficulties which led to the Revolutionary War.

Glynn County contains lands formerly included in the Colonial Parishes of St. David, St. Patrick, and St. James, which had been organized in 1758.

Among the early officials were the Hon. George Walton, Signer of the Declaration of Independence, Judge of the Superior Court; James Spalding, Alexander Bissett, Richard Leake, and Raymond Demere, Justices of the Inferior Court; John Goode, Clerk of the Inferior and Superior Courts; John Palmer, Sheriff; John Burnett, Register of Probates; Richard Bradley, Tax Collector; Martin Palmer, Tax Receiver; Joshua Miller, Surveyor; Jacob Helvestine, Coroner; George Handley (who in 1788 was elected Governor of the State of Georgia) and Christopher Hillary, Legislators; George Purvis, Richard Pritchard, Moses Burnett, John Piles, and John Burnett, Commissioners of Glynn Academy.

## GRADY COUNTY 1985

THIS COUNTY, CREATED BY ACT OF THE LEGISLATURE AUG. 17, 1905, IS NAMED for Henry W. Grady, nationally famous editor and "silver tongued orator" of the New South. Born in Athens, Ga., in 1850 and educated at the Universities of Georgia & Virginia, he died in 1889. Among the first County Officers were: Sheriff D. W. Tyus, Ordinary P. H. Herring, Clerk of Superior Court W. T. Crawford, Tax Receiver W. R. Wynn, Tax Collector R. W. Ponder, Treasurer M. G. McManus, Surveyor D. A. Jones, Coroner E. G. Harrell, School Commissioner J. B. Wight and Representative R. R. Terrell.

## GORDON COUNTY 1961

THIS COUNTY WAS NAMED FOR WILLIAM WASHINGTON GORDON, OF SAVANNAH (1796-1842). The first Georgian to graduate at West Point, he entered the practice of law and was a pioneer in the railroad field in this State.

He was the founder and first President of the Central Railroad and Banking Company, now the Central of Georgia System.

Gordon County was created by an act of the Georgia Legislature Feb. 13, 1850. Area 375 square miles. 1950 population 18,957.

# Greene County 1848-49

This County, created by Act of the Legislature Feb. 3, 1786, is named for Maj. Gen. Nathanael Greene, the strategist, who ranked second only to Gen. Washington. Born in Rhode Island in 1742, he died at his Georgia plantation in 1786. Seven miles north of Greensboro lies Penfield named for Josiah Penfield of Savannah who started the Fund to establish Mercer Institute there in 1833. The Institute was named for Jesse Mercer, leading Baptist divine of Georgia at that time. It received a Legislative Charter as Mercer University in 1837 and was moved to Macon after the War.

Gwinnett County 1885

## Habersham County 1963-64

Habersham County was created by Acts of the Legislature, Dec. 5, 1818, and named for Joseph Habersham (1751-1815), of Savannah, who had a summer home near Clarkesville. He served in the Revolution as a Lieut. Col. in the Ga. Continental line; was twice Speaker of the General Assembly; Mayor of Savannah, 1792-93; and Postmaster General of the United States, 1795-1801. The first Habersham County officers sworn in after the County was created were Miles Davis, Clerk of the Superior Court; Wm. B. Wofford, Sheriff; Joseph Dobson, Clerk of the Inferior Court; Wm. Steedly, Coroner; William Wofford, Sr., Surveyor; Benjamin Cleveland, Absalom Holcombe and James R. Wyly were sworn in as Members of the Inferior Court, Feb. 25, 1819, and Holcombe was succeeded by Arthur Alexander on April 20, 1819. James Allen, Benjamin Chastain, Absalom Holcombe, John Kiser, Thomas Brock, James O'Neal, Joseph Whitehead and John Bryan were sworn in as Justices of the Peace in 1821.

Cicero H. Sutton was the first Ordinary of Habersham County. Habersham County is noted for its healthful climate and beautiful scenery; its peaches and apples, and its fine schools.

## Hall County 1937

Lyman Hall (1725-90), one of three Georgia signers of the Declaration of Independence, was born in Connecticut but moved to Georgia when young. Member of the Savannah Conventions, 1774-75, and very influential in Georgia's joining in American Revolution; served in Colonial Congress from Parish of St. John, 1775-80. When British seized Georgia and confiscated his property, he and his family refuged in the north until 1782, when he returned to Georgia and served one term as Governor of the State.

He is buried under the Signers Monument in Augusta. Hall County (1818) was named for him.

HANCOCK COUNTY, CREATED BY ACT OF DEC. 17, 1793, WAS named for John Hancock of Mass., President of the Continental Congress and the first man to sign the Declaration of Independence. It has been the home of 4 Governors of Ga. – William Rabun, Charles James McDonald, William Jonathan Northen, Nathaniel Edwin

Harris. Among the first officers of Hancock County were: Thomas Lamar, Sheriff; William Pentecost, Clerk Inferior Court; Henry Graybill, Clerk Superior Court; Daniel Conner, Coroner; John Ragan, Surveyor; David Adams, Tax Collector; Samuel Goode and Richard Bonner, Tax Receivers.

# HANCOCK COUNTY 1881-83

# HARALSON COUNTY 1891-92

THIS COUNTY, CREATED BY ACT OF THE Legislature Jan. 26, 1856, is named for Gen. Hugh A. Haralson, Member of Congress and Chairman of the Committee on Military Affairs during the Mexican War. The County Site is named for James Buchanan, last Democratic President before the War. Among the first County Officers were: Sheriff John K. Holcombe, Clerk of Superior Court Van A. Brewster, Clerk of Inferior Court Jesse M. Jeams, Tax Receiver Hiram Ray, Tax Collector Alfred H. Green, Ordinary George H. Hamilton, Surveyor William D. F. Mann and Coroner John McClung.

HARRIS COUNTY 1908

## HEARD COUNTY 1964

THIS COUNTY, CREATED BY ACT OF THE Legislature December 22, 1830, is named for Hon. Stephen Heard, elected President of the Council Feb. 18, 1781, thus, in the absence of Gov. Howley, becoming Governor de facto. An Englishman who moved to Wilkes Co. from Virginia, Heard fought in the Revolution and distinguished himself at Kettle Creek. Among the first County Officers were: Clerk of Superior Court William Wood, Clerk of Inferior Court Paschal H. Taylor, Coroner David Cox and Surveyor Jackson Fitzpatrick. The first Sheriff, Jonathan Mewsick, was not commissioned until 1832.

## HART COUNTY 1971

HART COUNTY WAS CREATED BY THE LEGISLATURE ON DEC. 7, 1833 out of portions of Franklin and Elbert counties. It is the only county in Georgia named for a woman Nancy Hart.

Nancy Hart and her husband, Benjamin Hart, obtained a 400 acre grant 25 miles S. E. from Hartwell in Colonial days and erected a log cabin home. During the Revolutionary War six Tories forced their way into the Hart home and demanded that Nancy cook a meal for them. She started cooking an old turkey, meanwhile sending her daughter to the spring to blow a conch shell for help. Detected slipping the third Tory rifle through a crack in the wall, Nancy killed one of the Tories and wounded another. Hart and several neighbors, coming to her rescue, wanted to shoot the five surviving Tories but Nancy insisted that they be hanged,

and they were. Tradition has it that Nancy Hart served as a spy for Gen. Elijah Clarke, sometimes disguised as a man. The Indians respectfully called Nancy Hart "War Woman," giving that name to a creek adjacent to her cabin, which is memorialized in a State Park on State Highway Route 17.

Hart County's first officers elected in Feb. 1854 were Inferior Court Justices Henry F. Chandler, Micajah Carter, Clayton S. Webb, Daniel M. Johnson, James V. Richardson; Inferior Court Clerk Frederick C. Stephenson, Ordinary James T. Jones, Superior Court Clerk Burrell Mitchell, Sheriff William Myers, Tax Receiver W. C. Davis, Tax Collector Richard Shirley, Surveyor John A. Cameron, Coroner Richmond Skelton, and Treasurer Samuel White.

HENRY COUNTY 1897

IRWIN COUNTY 1910

*Opposite*

HOUSTON COUNTY 1948, 2005

*Above*

## Jackson County 1879

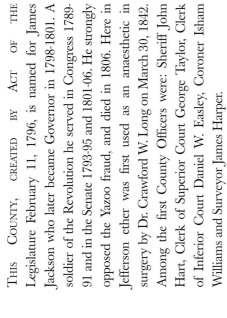

THIS COUNTY, CREATED BY ACT OF THE Legislature February 11, 1796, is named for James Jackson who later became Governor in 1798-1801. A soldier of the Revolution he served in Congress 1789-91 and in the Senate 1793-95 and 1801-06. He strongly opposed the Yazoo fraud, and died in 1806. Here in Jefferson ether was first used as an anaesthetic in surgery by Dr. Crawford W. Long on March 30, 1842. Among the first County Officers were: Sheriff John Hart, Clerk of Superior Court George Taylor, Clerk of Inferior Court Daniel W. Easley, Coroner Isham Williams and Surveyor James Harper.

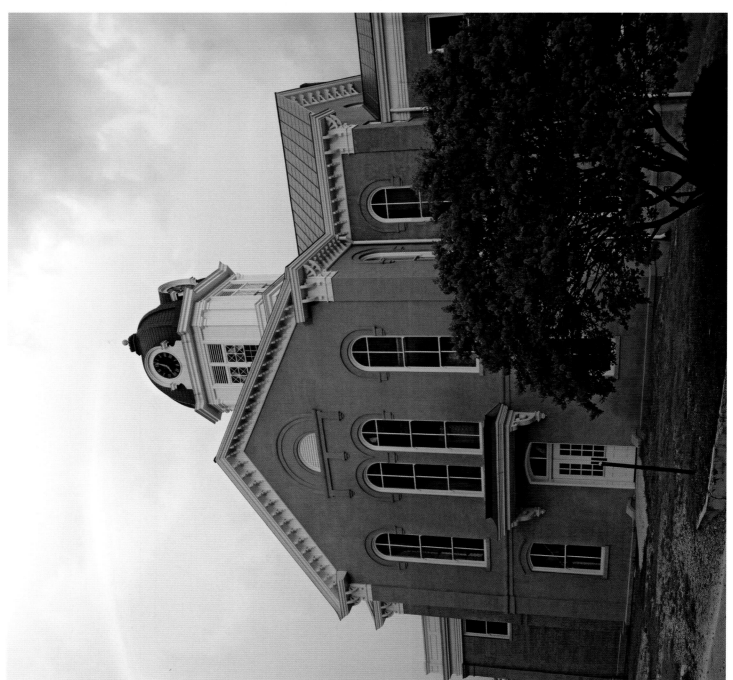

JASPER COUNTY 1907-08

## JEFF DAVIS COUNTY
### 1906-07, 1994-95

THIS COUNTY, CREATED BY ACT OF THE Legislature Aug. 18, 1905, is named for Jefferson Davis, President of the Confederacy. Born in Kentucky, Davis later moved to Mississippi. He was educated at Transylvania U. and West Point serving 7 years in the army partly under Gen. Zachary Taylor. Elected to Congress in '45, he again fought under Taylor at Monterey. He was appointed to the Senate in '47 & was Secretary of War under Pierce in '52. Elected President of the Confederacy in Sept. '61 he was captured by the Union Army at Irwinville, Ga. May 10, '65. He died in New Orleans December 6, 1889.

JEFFERSON COUNTY 1904

# JENKINS COUNTY 1910

JENKINS COUNTY WAS ORGANIZED FROM TERRITORY CUT from Burke, Screven, Bulloch, and Emanuel counties in 1905, and officially began its function as a new political unit on Jan. 1, 1906.

The first court house was completed in March, 1908 and burned Jan. 5, 1910. The present structure, essentially identical to the first, was rebuilt within the following two years. The building was designed by Lewis F. Goodrick of Augusta and its extravagant Italian Renaissance lines reflect something of the boundless optimism and pride of achievement of our early citizens.

JOHNSON COUNTY 1895

JONES COUNTY 1906

LAMAR COUNTY 1931

## LANIER COUNTY 1973

THIS COUNTY, CREATED BY ACTS OF THE LEGISLATURE AUG. 11, 1919 & AUG. 7 1920, is named for Sidney Lanier, poet of Georgia. Lanier was born in Macon Feb. 3, 1842 and practiced law there with his father after graduating from Oglethorpe Univ. then at Milledgeville. He married Mary Day of Macon in '67 after serving in the Confederate Army and being captured while commanding a blockade runner. In '73 he moved to Baltimore and lectured at Johns Hopkins. He died at Lynn, N. C. Sept. 7, 1881. Among his famous poems are "The Marshes of Glynn" & "Song of the Chatahoochee."

## LAURENS COUNTY 1962

LAURENS COUNTY WAS CREATED BY ACT OF DEC. 10, 1807 FROM WILKINSON COUNTY. Originally it contained all of Pulaski and part of Johnson Counties. Among prominent residents of Laurens County were Gov. Geo. M. Troup and Gen. David Blackshear. It was named for Col. John Laurens (1755-1782), aide-de-camp to Gen. Washington. He fought with gallantry at Brandywine, German-town, Monmouth, Savannah and Charleston. First officers of Laurens County commissioned Jan. 14, 1808, were: James Thompson, Sheriff; Amos Love, Clk. Sup. Ct.; James Yarborough, Clk. Inf. Ct.; John Thomas, Surveyor; William Yarborough, Coroner.

LEE COUNTY 1917-18

LIBERTY COUNTY 1926

*Above*

*Opposite*

LINCOLN COUNTY 1915

*Opposite*

LONG COUNTY 1926

*Above*

# LOWNDES COUNTY 1904-05

LOWNDES COUNTY WAS CREATED BY AN ACT OF THE Georgia Legislature December 23, 1825, from lands previously in Irwin County. It was named for William J. Lowndes, a South Carolina statesman. The first county officers commissioned May 29, 1826, were Henry Blair, Clerk of the Superior Court; William Smith, Ordinary; Norman Campbell, Tax Collector; William Hancock, Sheriff; Malachi Monk, Coroner; and Samuel M. Clyatt, Surveyor. The first state senator was William A. Knight and the first representative was Jonathan Knight for Lowndes County.

Lowndes County has had three county seats; Franklinville, Lowndesville (later changed to Troupville) and Valdosta.

LUMPKIN COUNTY 1836

Macon County 1894

# MADISON COUNTY 1901

THIS COUNTY, CREATED BY ACT OF THE Legislature December 5, 1811, is named for James Madison, Virginia Democrat, fourth President of the United States, 1809-17. The site for Danielsville was given by Gen. Allen Daniel of Revolutionary fame. In this town was born Dr. Crawford W. Long who first used ether in a surgical operation (1842). Among the first County Officers were: Sheriff Nathan Williford, Tax Receiver Britton Sanders Jr., Clerk of Superior Court James Long, Clerk of Inferior Court Samuel Williford, Tax Receiver Britton Sanders Jr., Tax Collector James Ware Jr., Coroner William Hodge and Surveyor Edward Ware Jr.

MARION COUNTY 1850, 1928

McDuffie County 1872

McIntosh County 1872

## MERIWETHER COUNTY 1904

MERIWETHER COUNTY, "SECOND HOME" OF PRES. FRANKLIN D. Roosevelt and birthplace of three Ga. Governors – Joseph M. Terrell, William Y. Atkinson, and John M. Slaton – was created by Act of Dec. 14, 1827 from Troup County. It was named for Gen. David Meriwether (1755-1823), Revolutionary soldier, legislator, Congressman. Representing the government in various negotiations with the Indians, he had unusual influence with their Chiefs. First officers of Meriwether County, commissioned Feb 7, 1828, were: Joseph Weaver, Sheriff; Hugh W. Ector, Clk. Sup. Ct.; A. M. Weathers, Clk. Inf. Ct.; Joseph Crockett, Surveyor; John Edmonds, Coroner.

## MILLER COUNTY 1977

THIS COUNTY, CREATED BY ACT OF THE LEGISLATURE FEBRUARY 26, 1856, IS NAMED for Judge Andrew J. Miller who died in 1856. A Commander of the Oglethorpe Infantry, he served in the legislature for more than twenty years and several times President of the Senate. He long championed a bill to give married women separate property rights. Among the first County Officers were: Sheriff Delmar Averett, Clerk of Superior & Inferior Courts Thomas S. Floyd, Ordinary Isaac Bush, Tax Receiver John Fiveash, Tax Collector West Sheffield and Surveyor James D. Pickern.

## MITCHELL COUNTY 1936-37

THIS COUNTY WAS CREATED BY AN ACT OF THE GEORGIA LEGISLATURE ON DEC. 21, 1857. Some historians say that the county was named for David. B. Mitchell, Governor of Georgia in 1809-13 and again in 1815-17, and that Camilla was named for his daughter. However, the Georgia Laws of 1857 (pages 38-40), creating Mitchell county, say the county was named in honor of Gen. Henry Mitchell, who was born in 1760 and died in 1839. He was a State Senator from Warren County, President of the Senate in 1809, President Elector in 1812, 1816 & 1820, and an outstanding Georgian. He was a Brigadier General of Georgia troops in the post-Revolutionary period.

The first officials of Mitchell County, who took office in 1858, were Sheriff Joshua P. Crosby; Ordinary John W. Pearce; Clerk of Superior Court Montford S. Poore; Clerk of Inferior Court Joseph T. Ellis; Tax Receiver John T. Allen; Tax Collector George West; Treasurer Nathan Maples; Surveyor Murdock McLeod, and Coroner William West. David West donated fifty acres of his land as a site for the Court House and Jail. A two story frame Court House was built in 1860 and replaced by the present brick building in 1890.

# MONROE COUNTY 1896

CREATED BY ACT OF MAY 15, 1821, MONROE COUNTY, an original county containing all of Pike, parts of Bibb, Butts and Lamar Counties, was ceded by the Creek Indians in early 1821. Laid out by the Lottery Act, it was rapidly occupied by large numbers of small landowners. The county was named for James Monroe, President of the U. S. (1817-1825). First officers, commissioned Apr. 1, 1822 were: John Cureton, Sheriff; Wilkins Hunt, Clk. Sup. Ct.; Isaac Welch, Clk. Inf. Ct.; John Tomlinson, Coroner; James Holloway, Surveyor, James Whatley became Surveyor, and Henry Jourdan, Coroner, on Sept. 17, 1822.

# MONTGOMERY COUNTY 1907

MONTGOMERY COUNTY, CREATED DEC. 19, 1793 OUT OF Washington, originally contained all of Wheeler and Tattnall and parts of Treutlen, Toombs, Emanuel and Dodge Counties. It was named for Maj. Gen. Richard Montgomery (1736-1775), "an early martyr to the cause of liberty." Commanding an expedition to Canada in 1775, he was killed at the Siege of Quebec. First County Officers, commissioned Feb. 17, 1794, were: March McKessak, Sheriff; Thos. Pugh, Clk. Inf. Ct.; Jonathan Eanmons, Clk. Sup. Ct.; Jonathan Holly, Cor.; Wm. Cawthorn, Reg. of Probate; Willis Wood, Sur.

# MORGAN COUNTY 1905

MORGAN COUNTY WAS CREATED BY ACT OF DEC. 10, 1807 from Baldwin County. It was named for Gen. Daniel Morgan (1736-1802), a native of N.J. "Exactly fitted for the toils and pomp of war," he served with distinction on Benedict Arnold's expedition to Quebec in 1775-6, commanded the riflemen at Saratoga in 1777 and defeated Tarleton at Cowpens in 1781. After the War he served two terms in Congress. First county officers of Morgan County, commissioned January 14, 1808, were: Joseph White, Sheriff; John Nesbitt, Clk. Sup. Ct.; Isham S. Fannen, Clk. Inf. Ct.; Daniel Sessions, Surveyor; Miles Gibbs, Coroner.

MURRAY COUNTY 1832

MUSCOGEE COUNTY 1972-73

115

NEWTON COUNTY 1884

# OCONEE COUNTY 1939

THIS COUNTY, CREATED BY ACT OF THE Legislature February 25, 1875, is named for the Oconee River which forms its eastern boundary. In 1801 Watkinsville was made County Site of Clarke County but in 1875 the Clarke County Site was changed to Athens. As a result indignant local citizens brought about the formation of Oconee County with Watkinsville as County Site. Among the first County Officer were: Sheriff Weldon M. Price, Clerk of Superior Court Jas. M. A. Johnson, Ordinary James R. Lyle, Tax Receiver David M. White, Tax Collector Robert R. Murray, Treasurer Thomas Booth, Coroner James Maulden and Surveyor Wm. E. Elder.

OGLETHORPE COUNTY 1887

PAUDLING COUNTY 1892

*Above*

*Opposite*

*Opposite*

THIS COUNTY, CREATED BY ACT OF THE LEGISLATURE July 18, 1924, is named for one of Georgia's leading crops, the Georgia Peach known throughout the nation and beyond. The famous Elberta Peach was developed in Georgia by Samuel B. Rumph and is grown widely in this area. Among the first County Officers were: Sheriff George D. Anderson, Clerk of Superior Court Emmett Houser, Ordinary M. C. Moseley, Tax Receiver C. N. Rountree, Tax Collector T. E. Tharpe, Treasurer C. E. Martin, Coroner W. H. Hafer and Surveyor T. F. Flournoy.

PICKENS COUNTY 1949

PIERCE COUNTY 1902

PIERCE COUNTY COURT HOUSE

# PIKE COUNTY 1895

CREATED BY ACT OF DEC. 9, 1822, FROM MONROE County, Pike County originally contained part of Spalding, Upson and Lamar Counties. It was named for Zebulon Montgomery Pike (1779-1813), leader, in 1805, of an expedition to trace the Mississippi River to its source. Later he explored the interior of Louisiana. Made a Brig. Gen. in 1813, he was killed in Toronto, Canada, while commanding American forces there. First officers of Pike County, commissioned Feb. 25, 1823, were: Willis Whatley, Sheriff; John H. Broadnax, Clk. Sup. Ct.; William Myrick, Clk. Inf. Ct.; Joel Moore, Coroner. James Lowery, Surveyor, was commissioned Jan. 9, 1824.

POLK COUNTY 1951

PULASKI COUNTY 1874

# PUTNAM COUNTY 1824, 1905-06

PUTNAM COUNTY WAS CREATED BY ACT OF DEC. 10, 1807 out of Baldwin County. Among the prominent men born in Putnam County were Joel Chandler Harris and L. Q. C. Lamar. It was named for General Israel Putnam (1718-1790), Massachusetts hero of the Revolution. He fought with the British in 1755 and in "Pontiac's War" in 1762. One of the leaders at the Battle of Bunker Hill, he was a gallant soldier and brave general. First officers of Putnam County, commissioned January 14, 1808, were: Samuel Reed, Sheriff; William Williams, Clk. Sup. Ct.; Landling Williams, Clk. Inf. Ct.; George Hill, Coroner.

# QUITMAN COUNTY 1939

COUNTY COURT HOUSE

THIS COUNTY, CREATED BY ACT OF THE LEGISLATURE Dec. 10, 1858, is named for Gen. John A. Quitman, soldier in the Mexican War, Governor of Mississippi and ardent advocate of States Rights. The County Site is named for Georgetown, D.C. Among the first County Officers were: Sheriff James M. Cooper, Clerk of Superior Court John R. M. Neel, Clerk of Inferior Court Joel A. Crawford, Ordinary Joel E. J. Smith, Tax Receiver James M. Granberry, Tax Collector Owen G. Thomas, Treasurer Nicholas T. Christian, Surveyor William J. Brown and Coroner Alden Hall.

# RABUN COUNTY 1967

THIS COUNTY CREATED BY ACT OF THE LEGISLATURE Dec. 21, 1819, is named for William Rabun, 11th Governor of Georgia who was elected in 1817 and died in 1819. Self-educated by reading he served as a member of the Legislature and as President of the Senate. Here now is located the famous Rabun Gap-Nacoochee School for the education of entire families. Among the first County Officers were: Justices of the Inferior Court Edward Coffee, John McClure, Samuel Farris, William Kelly, William Gillespie, Andrew Miller, James Dillard and Clerk Thomas Kelly.

## RANDOLPH COUNTY 1886

RANDOLPH COUNTY WAS CREATED BY ACT OF DEC. 20, 1828 from Lee County. Originally Randolph County included all of what is now Stewart and Quitman and part of Terrell and Clay Counties. It was named for "John Randolph of Roanoke" (1773-1833), Virginia statesman, for many years a member of the House of Representatives and Senate. He actively opposed the War of 1812 and the Missouri Compromise. First officers of this County, commissioned Jan. 12, 1830, were: Michael H. Hinch, Sheriff; Thomas R. Mangham, Clerk Superior Court; John M. Dennis, Clerk Inferior Court; Arnold E. Bloodworth, Surveyor; Joseph Day, Coroner.

# RICHMOND COUNTY 1956-57

ORIGINALLY DESIGNATED AS THE PARISH OF ST. PAUL BY the Act creating it in 1758, the name was changed in 1777 to Richmond County in honor of the Duke of Richmond, who, as a member of Parliament, was a zealous supporter of the American cause, advocating independence of the Colonies. It originally included a large part of four other counties: Columbia, Jefferson, McDuffie and Warren. Included within its borders are the incorporated towns of Augusta, the county seat; Hephzibah, formerly Brothersville; Blythe; and McBean.

Originally a trading community dealing in pelfry and tobacco, later its economy rested on numerous industries, principally textile, operated by power developed from its numerous creeks and the Augusta Canal constructed in 1845-1846, and agricultural products from rich arable farm lands. Numerous military engagements occurred here during the Revolutionary War, during which Augusta was twice captured by the British.

During the War Between the States, the United States Arsenal surrendered to State forces without resistance, and a Confederate powder factory, said to be the second largest then in existence, supplied the Confederate Army and Navy. United States Army encampments, McKenzie, Hancock and Gordon, maintained during the Spanish-American War, World War I and World War II, respectively.

## SCHLEY COUNTY 1899

THIS COUNTY, CREATED BY ACT OF THE LEGISLATURE DEC. 22, 1857, IS NAMED FOR William Schley, member of Congress 1833-35 and Governor 1835-37. Ellaville is named for Ella Burton, daughter of Robert Burton, who sold the land for the townsite. Nearby Pond Town was settled in 1812.

First county officers were: Ordinary Wm. J. May, Clerk Hiram L. French, Sheriff A.J. Womach, Tax Receiver Henry Scarborough, Tax Collector Henry D. Holt, Coroner Ben T. Smith, Representative Seaborn Hixon, State Senator Charles Edwards, Inferior Court Judges Johnson Springer, Jas. Murray, Robt. Burton, G. W. Johnson, R. W. Wilkinson.

## ROCKDALE COUNTY 1939

THIS COUNTY, CREATED BY ACT OF THE LEGISLATURE OCTOBER 18, 1870, IS NAMED FOR Rockdale Church, so called for the fine underlying granite strata. Conyers, the County Site, was incorporated in 1854 and named for a prominent physician. Smyrna Camp Ground, first Presbyterian camp ground in Georgia lies in this county. Among the first County Officers were: Sheriff I. W. Almand, Ordinary A. C. McCalla, Clerk of Superior Court F. J. Treadwell, Tax Receiver W. J. Green, Tax Collector F. W. Armistead, Treasurer M. F. Swan, Surveyor I. F. Albert and Coroner George Rodgers.

# SCREVEN COUNTY 1964

SCREVEN COUNTY WAS CREATED BY AN ACT OF THE General Assembly of Georgia, December 14th, 1793. It was named for General James Screven. The first county seat and court house was the home of Benjamin Lanier at what is now Rocky Ford.

In a companion Act the first county court officials were named as follows: Justices of Peace: Nathaniel Hudson, John Greene, Jr., Benjamin Richardson, Samuel Dunn, Robert Stafford, Luke Mizell, McKeen Greene, James Bevil, Joseph Plumer, Robert Williamson, Samuel Bird, John Loney, James Bird, James Williams, James H. Rutherford, Daniel Blackburn and William Pierce, Esquires.

The Justices of the Inferior Court named in the Act creating Screven County were: Benjamin Lanier, Caleb Howell, Lemuel Lanier, Paul Bevil and Drury Jones. In the first election held in Screven County, January 20th 1794, the following officers were elected: Sheriff, William Coursey; Clerk of the Superior Court, Thomas Hylton; Clerk of the Inferior Court, Robert Williams; Surveyor, Robert Stafford; Register of Probate, Lemuel Lanier; and Coroner, William Briger.

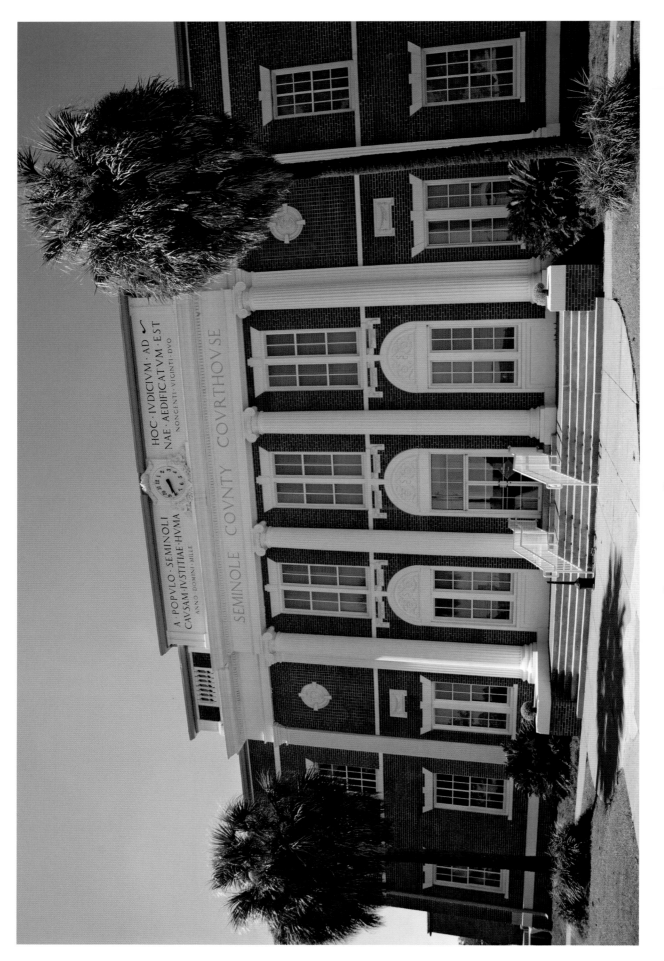

SEMINOLE COUNTY 1922

# SPALDING COUNTY

## SPALDING COUNTY 1985

SPALDING COUNTY WAS CREATED BY ACT OF DEC. 20, 1851 from Fayette, Henry and Pike Counties. It was named for Thomas Spalding (1774-1851), native of Frederica. One of the earliest cotton and sugar cane planters in Georgia, he was a legislator, state senator, Congressman, and member of the Constitutional Convention of 1798. First officers of Spalding County, commissioned Feb. 5, 1852, were: Addison A. Wooten, Sheriff; Henry B. Holliday, Clk. Sup. Ct.; James S. Wood, Clk. Inf. Ct.; William L. Gordon, Ord.; Elisha P. Bolton, Tax Rec.; Pressley Burdett, Tax Col.; Hezekiah Wheeler, Coroner; William Ellis, Surveyor.

# Stephens County 1908

This County, created by Act of the Legislature August 18, 1905, is named for Alexander Hamilton Stephens, Vice President of the Confederacy. A state legislator and Senator he was elected to Congress at 31, serving from 1843 to 1859. Elected to the Senate in 1866 he was refused his seat but again served in Congress from 1873 to '82 when he became Governor. He died March 4, 1883. Among the first County Officers were: Sheriff W. A. Bailey, Ordinary B. P. Brown Jr., Tax Receiver M. C. Jarrett, Tax Collector C. L. Mize, Treasurer C. H. Dance, Coroner Sidney Williams and Surveyor M. B. Collier.

STEWART COUNTY 1923

# SUMTER COUNTY 2010

THIS COUNTY, CREATED BY ACT OF THE LEGISLATURE December 26, 1831, is named for Gen. Thomas Sumter of South Carolina who fought in the French & Indian Wars and Revolution. At Andersonville was located the famous and unjustly criticized Confederate prison camp. Five miles N. East of Americus at Souther Field, Charles Lindbergh made his first solo Flight in 1923 in a newly purchased Gov't. surplus plane. Among the first County Officers were: Sheriff John Kimmey, Clerk of Superior Court Jacob W. Cobb, Clerk of Inferior Court Simmons C. Morgan and Coroner Larkin Glover.

# TALBOT COUNTY 1892

TALBOT COUNTY WAS CREATED BY ACT OF DEC. 14, 1827 from Muscogee County. Originally, it included part of Taylor County. It was named for Matthew Talbot (1767-1827), member of the legislature, member of the Convention that framed the Constitution of Ga., President of the State Senate, Governor in 1819 after the death of Gov. Rabun until the election of Gov. Clark. First officers of Talbot County, commissioned Feb. 9, 1828, were: Abraham Laurence, Sheriff; Samuel C. Leech, Clk. Sup. Ct.; William S. Goss, Clk. Inf. Ct.; Benjamin Loyd, Surveyor; Hubbard Brown, Coroner.

# Taliaferro County 1902

This County, created by an Act of the Legislature Dec. 24, 1825, is named for Colonel Benjamin Taliaferro, Revolutionary soldier in Lee's Legion and a member of Congress from 1799 to 1802. In this city stands Liberty Hall, now a State Shrine, beloved home in life and the last resting place of Alexander H. Stephens, affectionately known as "Little Alec" and "The Great Commoner."

Born in a log cabin in this county in 1812 and graduating from the University of Georgia in 1832, Mr. Stephens began his public career by serving six consecutive terms in the Georgia Legislature with distinction. He was elected to Congress in 1843 and served through 1859. He voted against secession in the Georgia Convention of 1861 but accepted his State's decision and was a delegate to the Montgomery convention at which the Confederacy was born. Elected Vice President of the Confederacy he served throughout the war, opposing many of the policies of President Jefferson Davis.

Mr. Stephens was elected to the United States Senate in 1866 but a seat was refused him. He was again elected to Congress in 1873 and served until 1882, when he was elected Governor of Georgia, dying in office on March 4, 1883.

Among Taliaferro County's first officers were: Sheriff Asa C. Alexander, Superior Court Clerk Marcus Andrews, Inferior Court Clerk Henry Perkins, Coroner Solomon Harper and Surveyor Henry Stewart.

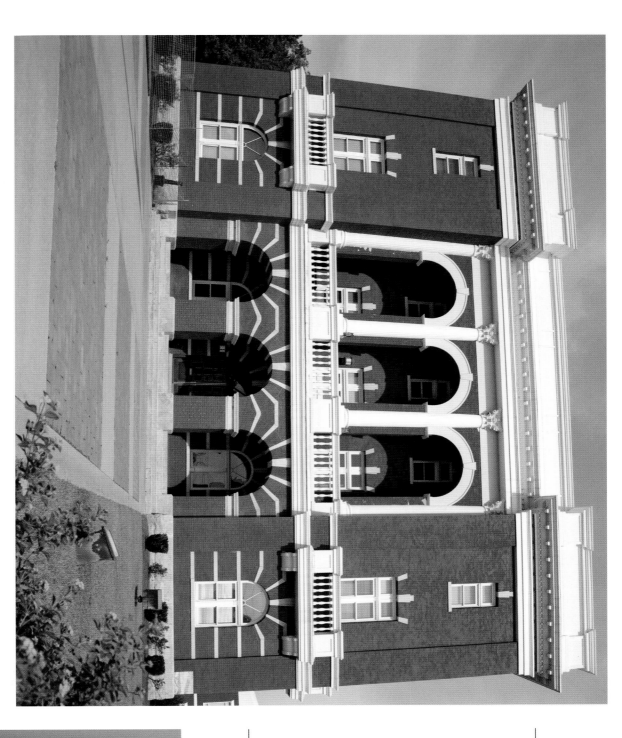

# TATTNALL COUNTY 1902

This County, created by Act of the Legislature Dec. 5, 1801, is named for Josiah Tattnall, Governor of Georgia at the time, who signed the Act. There being no town in the new County, the Act provided that all public business be transacted at the Zacharia Cox House on the Ohoopee River. In 1828 the Legislature named a Committee of seven men to select a site at the geographical center of the County for a Court House. When a Post Office was opened at this site in 1832, it was named Reidsville for Robert E. Reid, Judge of the Superior Court, later Territorial Governor of Florida.

Please DO NOT THROW CIGAR OR CIGARETTE BUTTS ON THE FLOOR
By Order of the Judge

# Taylor County 1935

Taylor County was created by Act of Jan. 15, 1852 from parts of Macon, Marion, and Talbot Counties. It was named for Zachary Taylor (1784-1850), 12th President of the U. S., Major-General, Commander of the Army of the Rio Grande. Known as "Old Rough and Ready," he captured Monterrey, Sept. 24, 1846 and defeated Santa Anna at Buena Vista, Feb. 22-23, 1847. First officers of Taylor County, commissioned July 24, 1852 were: J. M. Thompson, Sheriff; J. M. McCants, Clerk Sup. Ct.; James T. Harmon, Clerk Inf. Ct.; A. Rhodes, Tax Rec.; Charles Loyd, Tax Col.; J. B. Hamilton, Ordinary; C. Stewart, Coroner; Jonathan Stewart, Surveyor.

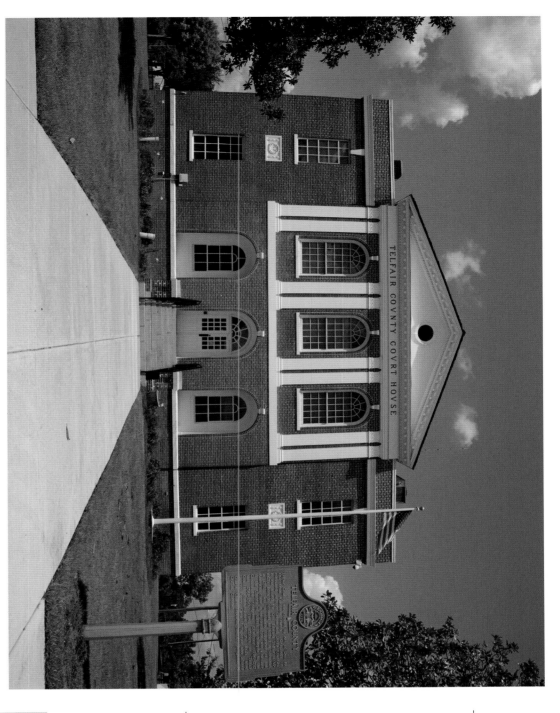

# Telfair County 1934

Telfair County was created by Act of Dec. 10, 1807 from Wilkinson County. Originally, it contained parts of Coffee and Dodge Counties. It was named for Gov. Edward Telfair (1735-1807). Born in Scotland, he settled in Savannah in 1766, was a staunch supporter of the American cause in the Revolution, was a member of the Council of Safety, a delegate to the Continental Congress. Governor 1786-1787 and 1790-1793. First officers of Telfair County, commissioned Dec. 20, 1808, were: Duncan Curry, Clerk of Superior and Inferior Courts; Cullen Edwards, Sheriff; Benjamin M. Griffin, Coroner.

# Terrell County 1892

This County, created by Act of the Legislature February 16, 1856, is named for Dr. William Terrell who died in 1855. He served in Congress from 1817 to '21. Eight miles west of here was fought the Battle of Echo-wa-noth-away Swamp in the Creek Indian War in 1836. Old Herod Town, an important Indian village, stood eight miles south. Among the first County Officers were: Sheriff Andrew I. Baldwin, Clerk of Superior Court Meyron Weston, Clerk of Inferior Court Daniel Lashley, Ordinary Ludwell M. Lennard, Tax Receiver Isaac Abbott, Tax Collector James W. Johnston, Coroner Bright W. Trewitt and Surveyor Daniel Lawken.

## THOMAS COUNTY 1858-1888

TIFT COUNTY 1912-13

## TOOMBS COUNTY 1964

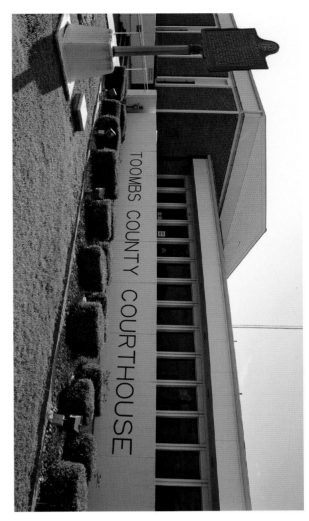

TOOMBS COUNTY WAS CREATED BY ACT OF AUG. 18, 1905 FROM EMANUEL, Montgomery and Tattnall. It was named for Gen. Robert Augustus Toombs (1810-1885), of Wilkes County, Congressman and Senator. One of the chief organizers of the Confederate government, he was Secretary of State and Brig. Gen. Bitterly opposed to Reconstruction, he never took the oath of allegiance after the war. First County Officers, commissioned Oct. 9, 1905, were: R. F. Scarboro, Sheriff; D. T. Gibbs, Clk. Sup. Ct.; R. J. Partin, Tax Rec.; O. V. Sharpe, Tax Col.; B. H. Grace, Sur.; M. D. Cowart, Cor.; John H. Clifton, Ord.; F. A. Thompson, Treas.

## TOWNS COUNTY 1964

TOWNS COUNTY WAS CREATED BY ACT OF MARCH 6, 1856 FROM RABUN AND UNION Counties. It was named for George Washington Towns, Governor of Georgia from 1847-1851. Gov. Towns was born in Wilkes County, May 4, 1801, of a Virginia family. Self-educated, he was a merchant, lawyer, legislator, state senator, Congressman. He died in 1854. First officers of Towns County, commissioned April 21, 1856, were: Andrew I. Burch, Sheriff; Martin L. Burch, Clerk Superior Court; James H. Moore, Clerk Inferior Court; Milton Brown, Tax Receiver; George M. Denton, Tax Collector; Robert S. Patton, Coroner; James Alston, Surveyor; John W. Holmes, Ordinary.

# TREUTLEN COUNTY 1920

TREUTLEN COUNTY WAS CREATED BY ACT OF AUG. 21, 1917 from Emanuel and Montgomery Counties. It was named for Gov. John Adam Treutlen (1726-1782), "one of the foremost revolutionists." Elected Governor over Button Gwinnett in 1777, he was declared a "rebel government" by the royal government and is believed to have been murdered by Tories in Orangeburg, S.C. First officers of Treutlen County, commissioned Dec. 9, 1918, were: M. B. Ware, Sheriff; N. L. Gillis, Ordinary: J. F. Mullis, Clk. Sup. Ct.; J. E. Thorpe, Tax Recc; W. M. Courson, Tax Col.; J. B. Dukes, Surveyor; A. Gillis, Treasurer; B. X. Watkins, Coroner; R. E. Ward, Sr., School Supt.

Troup County 1939

# TURNER COUNTY 1907

THIS COUNTY, CREATED BY ACT OF THE LEGISLATURE August 18, 1905, is named for Capt. Henry Gray Turner who was captured by Union troops at Gettysburg. A resident of Nashville and later of Quitman, he served in the legislature, and in Congress from 1881 to 1897. About 1855 the Battle of Sandy Sink was fought two miles east of Cool Springs with the Indians under Billy Bow Legs. Among the first County Officers were: Sheriff John B. Cason, Ordinary W. A. Greer, Clerk of Superior Court C. L. Royal, Tax Receiver V. A. Freeman, Tax Collector T. E. Brown and Treasurer J. H. Gorday.

TWIGGS COUNTY 1902-04

# Union County 1899

Union County was created by Act of Dec. 3, 1832 from Cherokee. Originally, it contained part of Fannin and Towns Counties. In 1832 there was much discussion over Union and States' rights. John Thomas, chosen by the people as a representative for the new County, when asked to suggest a name, is reported to have said, "Name it Union, for none but union-like men reside in it." First officers of Union County, commissioned March 20, 1833 were: James Crow, Sheriff; Arthur Gilbert, Clerk Superior Court; Joseph Jackson, Clerk Inferior Court; James Gaddis, Sr., Coroner; Joseph Chaffin, Surveyor.

UPSON COUNTY 1908

WALKER COUNTY 1917-19

Walton County 1884

# WARE COUNTY 1957

WARE COUNTY WAS CREATED OUT OF A PORTION OF Appling County by an Act of Dec. 25, 1824. It was named for United States Senator Nicholas Ware. Early in 1825 an Inferior Court was created, made up of Justices William Smith, Solomon Hall, John L. Stewart Jr., Philemon Bryan, Absalom Thomas. The first county officers elected in 1826 were William G. Henderson, Sheriff; Joseph Bryan, Superior Court Clerk; Zachariah Davis, Surveyor and Joshua Sharpe, Coroner. Philemon Bryan was the first State Senator and John L. Stewart first representative.

# WARREN COUNTY 1910, 2000

This County, created by Act of the Legislature Dec. 19, 1793, is named for Gen. Joseph Warren, Massachusetts Revolutionary hero killed at the Battle of Bunker Hill. What is claimed to have been the first iron works and woolen mills in Georgia was established by Col. Richard Bird at Ogeechee Falls near Georgetown. Among the first County Officers were: Sheriffs Peter Hodo & David Neal, Ordinary Septimus Weatherby, Clerks of Superior Court Wyche Goodwin & Isaiah Tucker, Clerk of Inferior Court Turner Persons, Surveyor Ethelred Thomas and Coroner John Trant.

WASHINGTON COUNTY 1868-69

# WAYNE COUNTY 1902-03

THIS COUNTY, CREATED BY ACTS OF THE LEGISLATURE May 11, 1803 and December 7, 1805, is named for Major General "Mad Anthony" Wayne, so called for his daring exploits in the Revolution. A Pennsylvanian, he fought in the South and was elected to Congress from Georgia in 1791 but after a contest the seat was declared vacant. The first County Site at Waynesville was too close to the border when Charlton County was cut off in 1854 and the Site was moved to Jesup, named for Gen. Jesup of the U. S. Army who rendered valuable service during the Creek War in 1836.

WEBSTER COUNTY 1915

WHEELER COUNTY 1917

## WHITE COUNTY 1859

WHITE COUNTY, CREATED BY ACT OF DEC. 22, 1857, was cut off from Habersham and Lumpkin Counties. Wm. H. Shelton, Repr. from Habersham at the session tried twice to have the county formed but failed. Repr. David T. White of Newton Co. backed the bill and it passed. In gratitude, Repr. Shelton had the county named for Repr. White. First county officers were: Isaac Bowen, Sheriff; Wm. L. Sumpter, Clk. Sup. Ct.; Wm. R. Kimsey, Clk. Inf. Ct.; Willis A. England, Cor.; Wm. Burke, Tax Rec.; Champion Ferguson, Tax Col.; Vincent F. Sears, Surveyor; Wilkes T. Leonard, Ord.; J. Cicero Bell, Treasurer.

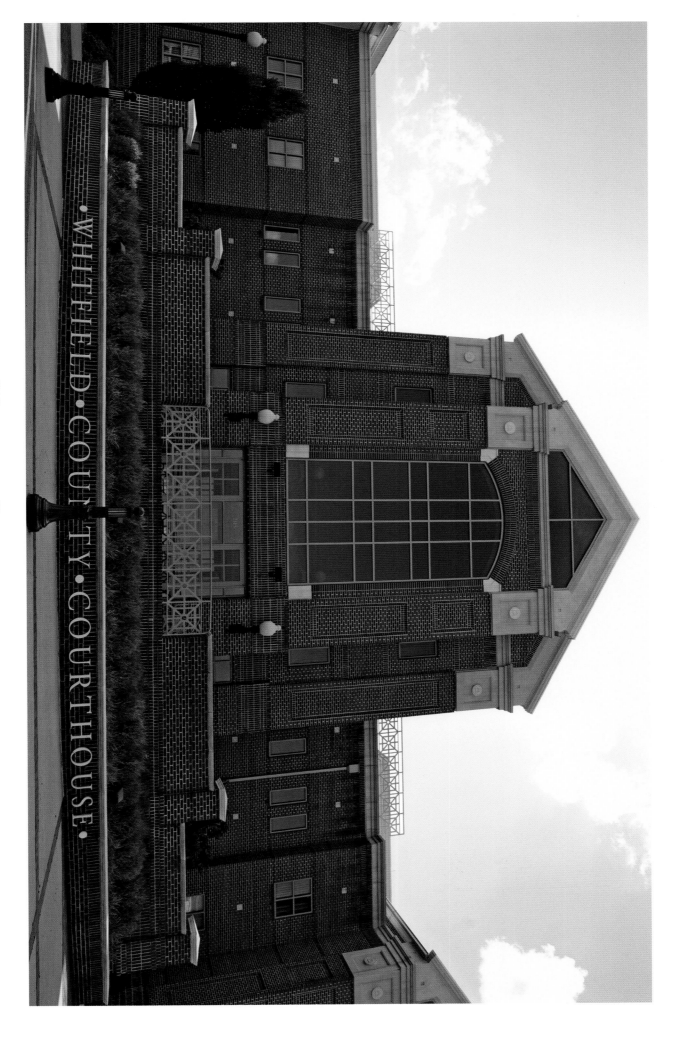

WHITFIELD·COUNTY·COURTHOUSE·

WHITFIELD COUNTY 2004-06

# WILCOX COUNTY 1903

THIS COUNTY WAS CREATED BY ACT OF THE LEGISLATURE DEC. 22, 1857. GEORGIA ARCHIVES show that it was named for Capt. John Wilcox though some authorities believe it was named for his son Gen. Mark Wilcox, state legislator and one of the founders of the Georgia Supreme Court, who died in 1850. Among the first County Officers were: Sheriff Joseph S. Graham, Clerk of Superior & Inferior Courts Stephen Bowen, Ordinary James W. Washburn, Tax Receiver John McCall, Tax Collector Stephen Mitchell, Surveyor William A. Barker and Coroner Daniel M. Bruce.

WILKES COUNTY 1904

# WILKINSON COUNTY 1924

THIS COUNTY WAS CREATED BY ACTS OF THE Legislature May 11, 1803 and Dec. 7, 1805. It is named for James Wilkinson, Revolutionary General, and formed from part of the lands acquired from the Creeks by the Treaty of Fort Wilkinson (on the Oconee) at which the General was a U. S. Commissioner. Irwinton, named for Gov. Jared Irwin, is located on the site of an English trading post that existed prior to 1715. Among the first County Officers were: Sheriff Edmund Hogan, Clerk of Superior Court Archibald McIntire; Clerk of Inferior Court William Brown; Ordinary Drury Gilbert, Tax Receiver Arthur Burney; Tax Collector William O'Neal; Coroner Charles Ray and Surveyor Britton McCullers.

COURTHOUSE

# WORTH COUNTY 1905

THIS COUNTY CREATED BY ACT OF THE LEGISLATURE Dec. 20, 1853 is named for Maj. Gen. Wm. J. Worth of Mexican War fame under whose command served Maj. William A. Harris, a leader in the organization of the new County. Among the first County Officers were: Sheriff James G. Brown, Clerk of Superior & Inferior Courts Wm. A. Johnston, Ordinary James M. Ford, Tax Receiver Jeremiah Spring, Tax Collector A. B. Mattox, Surveyor Thos. B. Arline, Coroner Jas. A. Olliver, State Senator Wm. A. Harris and State Representative M. Simmons.

# Additional Historical Marker Text

## Appling County

This County, created by Acts of the Legislature Dec. 15, 1818; Dec. 21, 1819 and Dec. 24,1824 is named for Colonel Daniel Appling who served in the War of 1812. Baxley was chosen as the County Site in 1874 and incorporated in 1875. The first Site, approved by the Legislature in 1828, was at Holmesville which was chartered in 1854. Among the first County Officers, who took office in 1820, were: Sheriff William Carter, Clerk of Superior and Inferior Courts John McAuley, Coroner James Mixon and Surveyor Daniel S. Whitehurst.

## Atkinson County

Atkinson County was created by an act of the Georgia legislature in 1917, out of lands previously in Clinch and Coffee Counties. The county was organized Jan. 1, 1918. The first officers were J. W. Roberts, Ordinary; Wiley M. Sumner, Clerk Superior Court; E. D. Leggett, Sheriff and Charles E. Stewart, Representative in legislature.

Members of the first Board of Commissioners, created in 1919, were Jeff Kirkland, David Weathers and J. M. Roberts Sr. The first Clerk to the Commissioners and County Attorney was L. A. Hargreaves.

## Bacon County

This County, created by Act of the Legislature July 27, 1914, is named for Augustus O. Bacon, four times U. S. Senator, who died in office Feb. 15, 1914. An expert on Mexican affairs, his death was a great loss coming at a time of critical relations with that nation. Born in 1839, Senator Bacon served as Adjutant of the 9th Georgia Regiment during the War of 61-65. Among the first County Officers were: Ordinary T. B. Taylor, Clerk of Superior Court Victor Deen, Sheriff J. W. Googe, Tax Collector J. N. Johnson, Tax Receiver L. W. Hutto, Treasurer J. G. Barber, Surveyor J. W. Medders and Coroner W. H. Lewis.

## Baker County

This County, created by Acts of the Legislature Dec. 12 & 24, 1825, is named for Col. John Baker of Revolutionary fame. The original County Site was at Byron but an Act of Dec. 26, 1831, established a new Site which was named Newton for Sgt. John Newton, a Revolutionary soldier. One of the hardest battles of the Creek Indian War was fought in Baker County at Chickasawhachee Creek in 1836. Among the first County Officers were: Sheriff Stafford Long, Clerk of Superior & Inferior Courts Thomas F. Whittington, Coroner John Gillion and Surveyor Jno. C. Neil.

## Brantley County

This County, created by Act of the Legislature Aug. 14, 1920, is named for Benjamin D. Brantley. It is said that the old B. & W. Railroad, which was partly destroyed, marked the most southern point of advance of Sherman's Army. Among the first County Officers were: Sheriff W. H. Howard, Ordinary Wm. M. Roberson, Clerk of Superior Court John R. James, Tax Receiver Isaac E. Highsmith, Tax Collector M. H. Robinson, Treasurer W. T. Purdom, Coroner Dr. D. L. Moore and Surveyor D. H. Raulerson.

## Brooks County

This County created by Act of the Legislature Dec. 11, 1858, is named for Preston Smith Brooks, zealous defender of States Rights. Born in S. C. Aug. 6, 1819, Brookes served in the Mexican War & in Congress. He died June 27, 1857. The first County Officers included: Ordinary Angus Morrison, Sheriff Enoch Hall Pike, Clerk of Superior & Inferior Courts D. W. McRae, Tax Collector Georgia Alderman, Tax Receiver John Delk, Treasurer William F. Speight, Surveyor Jeremiah Wilson, Coroner John T. Devane, State Senator Shadrack Griffin and Representative John T. Edmondson.

## Bryan County

This County created by Act of the Legislature Dec. 19, 1793, is named for Jonathan Bryan, Revolutionary patriot and member of the Executive Council in 1777. The "lost town" of Hardwick on the Ogeechee River was the first temporary County Site. Laid out in 1755, it was named for Lord Hardwick, Lord Chancellor of England, a relative of the then Gov. Reynolds. Two Royal Governors recommended that it be the Capital of Georgia. An Act of 1797 designated a new County Site at Cross Roads, 2 miles from Ogeechee Bridge. The Site was later moved to Clyde and then Pembroke.

## Burke County

Burke County, an original county, was created by the Const. of Feb. 5, 1777, from Creek Cession of May 30, 1733. In 1758, it had been organized as the Parish of St. George. Originally, it contained parts of Jefferson, Jenkins and Screven Counties. Burke County was named for Edmund Burke (1729-1797), writer, member of Parliament and eloquent defender of the cause of the colonies in America. Lemuel Lanier was commissioned Sheriff, Jan. 27, 1778. Thos. Burton, David Lewis, Nathan Hooker, Dan. McMurphy became Tax Collectors in 1778. Thos. Lewis, Jr., was made Surveyor Feb. 17, 1782. In 1787 John Davies was commissioned Clerk of Courts and John Duhart, Coroner.

## Camden County

Formed from old Colonial parishes: St. Mary and St Thomas. Camden one of eight original counties of Georgia created by the State Constitution of 1777. County named for Charles Pratt, Earl of Camden, Chief Justice and Lord Chancellor of England. Camden County gave territory to Wayne in 1808 and 1812, and to Charlton in 1854. St. Marys was temporary County Site until Jefferson (Jeffersonton) was named as first permanent county site by an Act of Nov. 29, 1800. Jefferson seat of government sixty-nine years (1801-1871). Election held Jan. 3, 1871, authorized county seat be removed from Jefferson to St. Marys. St. Marys county seat for fifty-two years (1871-1923). Act of Aug. 11, 1923 authorized removal of county seat from St. Marys to Woodbine. Present courthouse here erected 1928.

Some of the first and early settlers of the county were: Talmadge Hall, James Woodland, Thomas Stafford, David & Hugh Brown, John King, John Hardee, Henry Osborne, Jacob Weed, John Webb, Abner Williams, Charles & John Floyd, Nathan Atkinson, Isaac & Richard Lang, Joseph Hull, William Berrie, Thomas Miller, John Bailey, Sr., and nephew, John Bailey, and Lewis DuFour.

First County offices were: Alexander Semple, Clerk of Court; Wilson Williams, Sheriff; John Crawford, Coroner; Nathaniel Ashley, Tax Col.; Robert Brown, Register of Probates.

A number of the early settlers of this county came from Acadia, San Domingo, Minorca, and Spanish East Florida.

## Clinch County

Clinch County was created by an Act of the Legislature approved Feb. 14, 1850 out of lands formerly in Lowndes and Ware Counties and was named for General Duncan L. Clinch, a hero of the War of 1812 and the Indian wars. At the first election held in April, 1850, J. C. Kirkland was elected clerk of the Superior and Inferior Courts; Charles Cowart, sheriff; Benjamin Cornelius, tax receiver; Ezekiel J. Sirmans, tax collector; David J. Blackburn, surveyor; Joseph L. Rogers, coroner; David Johnson, Hiram Sears and Manning Smith, justices of the Inferior Court.

## Colquitt County

This County, created by Act of the Legislature February 25, 1856, is named for Hon. Walter T. Colquitt who had recently died. A famous lawyer and Methodist preacher, he served in Congress in 1839-40 and 1842-43, and in the Senate from 1843 to '48. "As an advocate Judge Colquitt stood alone in Georgia." Among the first County Officers were: Sheriff Jacob F. Reichert, Clerk of Superior Court William McLeod, Ordinary Hardy Chastain, Tax Receiver John A. Alderman, Tax Collector Job Turner, Coroner Elijah Tillman and Surveyor Amos Turner.

## COLUMBIA COUNTY

COLUMBIA COUNTY, NAMED FOR CHRISTOPHER COLUMBUS, WAS CREATED BY Act of Dec. 10, 1790 from Richmond County. Originally, it contained parts of McDuffie and Warren Counties. Settled by Quakers before the Revolution, it has been the home of many prominent Georgians. Here were Carmel Academy and Kiokee Baptist Church, "Mother Church" of Baptists in Georgia. First officers of Columbia County, commissioned Dec. 15, 1790, were: John Pearre, Coroner; John Walton, Surveyor; Daniel Marshall, Tax Col.; Anderson Crawford, Tax Rec.; Edmund B. Jenkins, Sheriff.

## COOK COUNTY

This COUNTY, CREATED BY ACT OF THE LEGISLATURE JULY 30, 1918, IS NAMED for Gen. Philip Cook who fought in the States and Seminole Wars. He served in Congress from 1872 to '82, was Secretary of State for Georgia 1890-94 and 1898-1918. He served as one of five Commissioners to erect the present State Capitol. Among the first County Officers were: Sheriff W.T. Dougherty, Ordinary C. O. Smith, Clerk of Superior Court F. R. Booth, Tax Receiver J. A. Kinnard, Tax Collector J. B. Wright, Treasurer W. M. Tyson, Surveyor E. R. Slade and Coroner A. D. Wiseman.

## DAWSON COUNTY

This COUNTY, CREATED BY ACT OF THE LEGISLATURE DEC. 3, 1857, IS NAMED for William C. Dawson who died in 1856, having served in Congress from Dec. 1836 to Nov. 1842, and in the U. S. Senate from 1849 to 1855. He also commanded a brigade in the Creek Indian War of 1836. Among the first County Officers were: Sheriff Samuel R. Fendley, Ordinary Henry K. Mikel, Clerk of Superior Court Daniel P. Monroe, Clerk of Inferior Court John Matthews, Tax Receiver David H. Logan, Tax Collector John Bruce, Treasurer James B. Gordon, Surveyor Andrew I. Glenn and Coroner John W. Beck.

## DEKALB COUNTY

DEKALB COUNTY, CREATED BY ACT OF GENERAL ASSEMBLY DEC. 9, 1822 AND including Fulton County until 1853, was named for Baron Johann DeKalb, a native German who fought gallantly for American freedom. Wounded and captured at the Battle of Camden, S. C., August 9, 1780, he died a British prisoner. Most of the early settlers of DeKalb County came from Virginia, North Carolina, South Carolina. First County Officers, commissioned March 18, 1822 in Fayette County, were: John S. Welch, Sheriff; Thomas A. Dobbs, Clerk Superior Court; Jonathan Dobbs, Clerk Inferior Court; John Calhoun, Coroner; James Adams, Surveyor.

## DODGE COUNTY

This COUNTY CREATED BY ACT OF THE LEGISLATURE OCT. 26, 1870, IS NAMED for William E. Dodge, a New York lumberman who owned large areas of the forest lands and who persuaded Congress to remove taxation from "the great staple of our state." He built and gave to the new county its first Courthouse, which was replaced in 1908. The first County Officers included: Superior Court Judge J. R. Alexander, Clerk of Superior Court Ruben A. Harrell, Sheriff Jordan Brown, Tax Collector T. P. Willcox, Tax Receiver Jno. W. Bohannon and Ordinary S. W. Burch.

## EARLY COUNTY

EARLY COUNTY, AN ORIGINAL COUNTY, WAS CREATED BY ACT OF DEC. 15, 1818, from Creek Cession of Aug. 9, 1814. At first it contained Decatur, Seminole, Baker, Mitchell, Calhoun, Miller, Dougherty and parts of Clay, Grady, and Thomas Counties. It was named for Peter Early (1773-1817), judge, state senator, Governor, Congressman. First County Officers, commissioned May 18, 1820, were: Thomas Taylor, Clk. Sup. Ct.; Otheniel Weaver, Clk. Inf. Ct.; Charles Thigpen, Sur.; Mark Cole, Cor.; John Dill, Tax Rec.; Jefferson Nichols, Tax Col. John Brockman became Sheriff in July, 1820.

## EFFINGHAM COUNTY

THIS IS ONE OF THE EIGHT ORIGINAL COUNTIES CREATED BY THE GEORGIA Constitution in 1777 and is named for Lord Effingham who was an ardent supporter of Colonial Rights. By Act of Feb. 26, 1784, the first County Site was located at Tuckasee-King near the Screven Co. line. From 1787 to '96 the Site was at Elberton on the North side of the Ogeechee near Indian Bluff. The Legislature meeting at Louisville Feb. 7, 1799 appointed five Commissioners to lay out a new Site which became the town of Effingham. The Site was later moved to Springfield, incorporated in 1838.

## ELBERT COUNTY

CREATED FROM WILKES COUNTY BY ACT OF DEC. 10, 1790, ELBERT COUNTY was settled in 1784 by Gen. George Mathews and a group from Virginia and Carolina. The site of Petersburg, the original settlement and third largest town in Georgia in its day, is covered by the Clark Hill Reservoir. Nancy Hart, celebrated Revolutionary patriot, lived in this county. Elbert County was named for Gen. Samuel Elbert, Revolutionary soldier and Governor of Georgia (1785-1786). A native of South Carolina and resident of Savannah (1778), he was a member of the Council of Safety and fought at and Brier Creek (1779).

On Jan. 20, 1791, the first session of Elbert County Superior Court was held at the home of Thos. A. Carter on Beaverdam Creek, some 5 miles NW of here. George Walton, Georgia signer of the Declaration of Independence, was presiding judge. The Carter plantation house stands today; Nearby is the family cemetery. First officers of Elbert County were: Matthew Talbot, Clerk; Robert Middleton, Sheriff; Robert Cosby, Collector of Taxes; W. Higginbottom, Register of Probate; Thos. Burton, Receiver of Tax Returns; Richardson Hunt, Surveyor; James Tate, Coroner.

## EMANUEL COUNTY

This COUNTY, CREATED BY ACTS OF THE LEGISLATURE DECEMBER 10, 1812 & December 6, 1813, is named for David Emanuel, Governor in 1801, several times a legislator, and President of the Senate. A place 1 mile from the center of the County was designated as County Site in 1814 and named Swainsboro for a prominent local family in 1822. The name was changed to Paris in 1854 but the original name was later revived. Among the first County Officers were: Sheriff Josiah Whitney, Clerk of Superior & Inferior Courts Stephen Rich and Tax Collector & Receiver James Fitzgerald.

## FANNIN COUNTY

THIS COUNTY, CREATED BY ACT OF THE LEGISLATURE JAN. 21, 1854, IS NAMED for Col. J. W. Fannin who was killed in the massacre at Goliad, Mar. 27, 1836. He had been captured with about 350 Georgia Volunteers under his command while fighting for the Republic of Texas in its successful War of Independence with Mexico. The first County Site was at Morganton, but it was moved to Blue Ridge Aug. 13, 1895 by vote of a public election. The greater part of this County, which contains the Noontootly National Game Refuge, lies in the Chattahoochee National Forest.

## FORSYTH COUNTY

FORSYTH COUNTY WAS CREATED BY ACT OF DEC. 3, 1832 FROM CHEROKEE County. It was named for Gov. John Forsyth (1780-1841), a native of Frederick Co., Va., a graduate of Princeton, and gifted Georgia lawyer. He was Attorney General of Ga., Congressman, Senator, Minister to Spain, Governor, and Secretary of State under Presidents Jackson and Van Buren. First officers of Forsyth County, commissioned April 20, 1833, were: John Blaylock, Clerk of Superior Court; Thomas Burford, County Surveyor; Alston B. Wilborn, Coroner. Hubbard Barker was commissioned Sheriff, January 31, 1834.

## FRANKLIN COUNTY

THIS COUNTY, CREATED BY ACT OF THE LEGISLATURE FEB. 25, 1784, IS NAMED for Benjamin Franklin, Revolutionary patriot and statesman. It was formed from lands obtained from the Indians by the Treaty of Augusta, 1783. Capt. James Terrell of the Revolution was an early settler. Volunteers from Franklin Co. under Capt. Morris distinguished themselves at the Battle of Pea River Swamp, Mar. 25, 1837, in the Creek Indian War. The present County Site was established by Act of Nov. 29, 1806, at Carnesville named for Thomas B. Carnes, member of the Third Congress, 1793-'97.

## GILMER COUNTY

GILMER COUNTY WAS CREATED BY ACT OF DEC. 3, 1832 OUT OF CHEROKEE. Originally, it contained parts of Fannin, Dawson and Pickens Counties. The county was named for George Rockingham Gilmer (1790-1859), who served with distinction as a soldier, lawyer, legislator, Congressman and twice as Governor of Georgia, 1829-1831 and 1837-1839. First officers, commissioned March 9, 1833, were: Levi A. Hufsteller, Sheriff; Thomas M. Burnett, Clerk Superior Court; Henry K. Quillian, Clerk Inferior Court. Officers commissioned July 10, 1833 were Thomas Gutterry, Coroner; and Benjamin M. Griffith, Surveyor.

## GWINNETT COUNTY

CREATED IN 1818 FROM CHEROKEE AND CREEK CESSIONS, GWINNETT IS AN original county. Courts, elections, and sheriff sales were held, first, in the home of Elisha Winn, 1 mile east of the Appalachee River. Selected to buy a permanent site for the county town. Winn purchased Lot 146, consisting of 250 acres in the Fifth Land District, for $200 from John Breedlove of Hancock County who had drawn it in the lottery.

First County Officers, commissioned in March, 1819, were: William Blake, Sheriff; James Wardlaw, Clerk Superior Court; Thomas A. Dobbs, Clerk Inferior Court; John Wynn, Corner; James C. Reed, Surveyor; James Loughridge, Tax Collector; John W. Beauchamp, Tax Receiver.

In 1849, the four corner lots on the public square were deeded to Charles H. Smith (Bill Arp). N. L. Hutchins, James P. Simmons, and T. W. Alexander; lawyers, so long as they maintained a substantial fence around the square to keep out wandering livestock. The first fence under this agreement was eight feet high with a stile on each side.

## HARRIS COUNTY

THIS COUNTY, CREATED BY ACTS OF THE LEGISLATURE DEC. 14 & 24, 1827, IS named for Charles Harris, eminent Savannah jurist. Born in England and educated in France, he served Savannah as Alderman or Mayor for 20 years, refusing higher offices. The first Court House was built in 1831 and the present one in 1908. First election was held in Feb. 1828. First county officers were: Sheriff Lewis Wynn, Superior Court Clerk Clark Blandford, Inferior Court Clerk Josiah W. Batchelder, Surveyor Absalom Beddell, Coroner F. A. B. Wheeler, Tax Receiver Burrell Blackmon, Tax Collector John D. Johnson.

## HENRY COUNTY

THIS COUNTY, CREATED BY ACTS OF THE LEGISLATURE MAY 15 & DECEMBER 24, 1821, is named for Patrick Henry, Revolutionary patriot, orator and statesman, largely responsible for the Bill of Rights and known best for his words "Give me liberty or give me death." At Sharon Church seven miles east

of here, founded Feb. 28, 1824, occurred the split between the Primitive and Missionary Baptists in Georgia. Among the first County Officers were: Sheriff James Fletcher, Clerk of Superior Court William Hardin, Clerk of Inferior Court John M. Forbes, Surveyor Wylie Ferrell and Coroner William Missor.

## HOUSTON COUNTY

THIS COUNTY, CREATED BY ACTS OF THE LEGISLATURE MAY 15 & DECEMBER 24, 1821, is named for John Houston, Governor in 1778 & 1784, who served in the Continental Congress in 1775 & '76. In 1774 he called the first meeting of the Sons of Liberty and served as Chairman. As Governor he invaded East Florida with Maj. Gen. Robert Howe in an unsuccessful attempt to take St. Augustine from the British. Among the first County Officers were: Sheriff Edmund C. Beard, Clerk of Superior Court Alexander McCarty, Clerk of Inferior Court Lawson I. Keener, Coroner Henry Audulph and Surveyor Simon Harrell.

## IRWIN COUNTY

THIS COUNTY, CREATED BY ACTS OF THE LEGISLATURE DECEMBER 15, 1818 and December 21,1819, is named for Gov. Jared Irwin who served from 1806 to '09. He helped revised the State Constitution in 1789 and '98 and was famed for his uncompromising opposition to the Yazoo fraud. Jefferson Davis, President of the Confederacy, was captured by Union soldiers near Irwinville, where his party had camped for the night May 10, 1865. Among the first County Officers were: Sheriff James Allen, Clerk of Superior Court William Stone, Tax Receiver William Hall, Tax Collector Redding Hunter and Coroner David Hunter.

## JASPER COUNTY

THIS COUNTY, CREATED BY ACTS OF THE LEGISLATURE DEC. 10, 1807, IS named for Sergeant Jasper, Revolutionary hero from South Carolina who rescued some American prisoners from their British guards at Jasper Spring, near Savannah. He was later killed in the siege of Savannah. When created, the County was named Randolph for John Randolph, Virginia statesman, whose later views on the War of 1812 made him unpopular in Georgia and resulted in the changing of the name to Jasper by Act of Dec. 10, 1812. Subsequently a new county was named for Randolph in 1828.

## JOHNSON COUNTY

THIS COUNTY, CREATED BY ACT OF THE LEGISLATURE DEC. 11, 1858, IS NAMED for Gov. Herschel V. Johnson. The County Site is named for John B. Wright, pioneer resident. Johnson, Governor from 1853 to '57, ran for the Vice Presidency in 1860 on the ticket with Stephen A. Douglas of Illinois. Among the first County Officers were: Sheriff Joshua Hightower, Ordinary

Theophilus Christian, Clerk of Superior Court James W. Walker, Clerk of Inferior Court Richard Walker, Tax Receiver Madison H. Mason, Tax Collector Jacob T. Snell, Surveyor Wm. B. Snell and Coroner George W. Hammock.

## JONES COUNTY

THIS COUNTY, CREATED BY ACT OF THE LEGISLATURE DEC. 10, 1807, IS NAMED for James Jones of Savannah, a legislator at 23 and member of the State Constitutional Convention in 1798 in which year he was elected to Congress. The first County Site was at Clinton but it was changed to Gray in 1905. Among the first County Officers were: Sheriff James Riley, Clerk of Superior Court John R. Gregory, Clerk of Inferior Court James Bond, Tax Receiver Daniel Candler, Tax Collector Hillery Pratt, Coroner Thomas Thrower and Surveyor Charles Miller. First Justices of the Inferior Court were: William Binion, William Jones, Hugh M. Comer, James Jackson and John McKenzie.

## LAMAR COUNTY

LAMAR COUNTY WAS CREATED BY ACT OF STATE ASSEMBLY AUGUST 17, 1920.

It was named for Lucius Quintus Cincinnatus Lamar, lawyer, Colonel in the Confederate Army, U. S. Senator, Secretary of the Interior and Justice of the U. S. Supreme Court. The first officers of Lamar County included: B. H. Hardy, Ordinary; S. J.Childers, Clerk of Court; Z. T. Elliott, Sheriff; E. Luther Butler, Tax Receiver; Gus Smith Tax Collector; W. C. Jordan, Treasurer; B. K. Crouch, Coroner; Roger H. Taylor, Surveyor; J. F. Redding, Judge; Mrs. Mattie Barnes, School Supt.; H. M. Johnson, E.O. Dobbs, H. J. Kennedy, Solicitors.

## LEE COUNTY

LEE COUNTY WAS CREATED BY ACTS OF JUNE 9, 1825 AND DEC. 11, 1826 FROM Creek cessions of Jan. 24, 1826 and March 31, 1826. Originally, it contained all land in Randolph, Stewart, Quitman, Sumter, Terrell, Webster and part of Marion and Clay Counties. Lee County was named for Richard Henry Lee (1732-1794), Virginia Congressman, who on June 7, 1776 moved "that the colonies declare themselves free and independent." First officers, commissioned May 14, 1827, were: Nathan Powell, Sheriff; Joseph White, Clerk of Sup. and Inf. Courts. Commissioned August 26, 1828 were Abner Holliday, Surveyor, and Gabriel Parker, Coroner.

## LIBERTY COUNTY

LIBERTY COUNTY, AN ORIGINAL COUNTY, WAS CREATED BY THE CONSTITUTION of Feb. 5, 1777 from Creek Cession of May 20, 1733. It had been organized in 1758 as the Parishes of St. John, St. Andrew and St. James. The theatre of many important events during the Revolution, Liberty County was named for American Independence. From it all of Long and McIntosh Counties were formed. Samuel Morecock was commissioned Sheriff in 1778. Wm. Barnard became Surveyor, Feb. 17, 1782. Francis Coddington in 1785 was made Clerk of Inf. and Sup. Courts of Liberty, Glynn and Camden Counties. John Lawson was sworn in as Coroner in 1790.

## LINCOLN COUNTY

LINCOLN COUNTY WAS CREATED BY ACT OF FEB. 20, 1796 FROM WILKES County. It was named for Maj. Gen. Benjamin Lincoln (1733-1810) of Hingham, Mass., who held the Chief Command of the Southern Department in the Continental Army. In 1781 he became Secy. of War. In 1789 he was appointed Collector of the Port of Boston. First County Officers, commissioned Sep. 15, 1796, were: James Hughes, Sheriff; Wm. Dowsing, Clerk, Inf. Court; Abner Tatom, Clerk Sup. Court; Britain Lockhart, Coroner; Joel Lockhart, Surveyor; John Middleton, Reg. of Probate. In 1798 John Seale became Tax Col. and Edward Smith, Tax Rec.

## LONG COUNTY

THIS COUNTY, CREATED BY ACT OF THE LEGISLATURE AUGUST 14, 1920, is named for Dr. Crawford W. Long who first used ether as an anaesthetic in a surgical operation, at Jefferson, Ga., March 30, 1842. Born in Danielsville Nov. 1, 1815, Dr. Long was a graduate of Franklin College (now U. of Ga.). Among the first County Officers were: Sheriff W. R. Wilkinson, Clerk of Superior Court C. W. Dawson, Ordinary T. J. Harrington, Tax Receiver J. McI. Cameron, Tax Collector T. H. Smiley, Treasurer R. D. Easterling, Coroner L. M. Branch and Surveyor M. C. Sarrason.

## MACON COUNTY

This COUNTY, CREATED BY ACT OF THE LEGISLATURE DEC. 14, 1837, IS NAMED for Nathaniel Macon of North Carolina, President Pro-Tem of the U. S. Senate. The first County Site at Lanier was moved to Oglethorpe in 1854 to be on the railroad. Lanier became a "lost town" as did Travelers Rest whose people moved to the railroad at Montezuma two miles away. There was an unsuccessful effort in 1893 to move the County Site to Montezuma. At Willow Lake in this County Sam Rumph and his son Sam Henry Rumph developed the famous Elberta peach named for the latter's wife.

## MARION COUNTY

MARION COUNTY NEW COURTHOUSE – 1850 BUILT IN 1850 OF LOCALLY MADE brick, this is one of two courthouses standing in Marion County. The other built in 1848 is at Tazewell. The first courthouse was at Horry. When the county seat was moved here the town was called Pea Ridge. Wishing a new name the citizens chose Taylor, for Gen. Zach Taylor, but found there was already a Taylor, Ga. Then came news of a Mexican War victory at Buena Vista and this name was chosen. Pea Ridge was one mile from the ancient Indian village of King's Town on the Uchee Trail used by Indians to carry trading goods 300 miles from Alabama to Savannah.

MARION COUNTY OLD COURTHOUSE – 1848 This COURTHOUSE BUILT IN 1848 at a cost of $1,637 replaced one built in 1839 and burned in 1845. The courthouse now in use was built at Buena Vista, then Pea Ridge, in 1850 when the county seat was moved. The first courthouse was at Horry. Members of Marion Lodge No. 14 F. & A. M. established in 1840 have met in this old courthouse since its construction. Prior to this they met in the courthouse that was burned. This courthouse now marks the exact center of the new city limits established by incorporation in 1953.

## McDUFFIE COUNTY

McDuffie COUNTY WAS CREATED BY ACT OF OCT. 18, 1870 FROM COLUMBIA and Warren Counties. It was named for George McDuffie (1788-1851). Born in Columbia (now Warren County, Ga.), he became a political leader in S. C. He was a Maj. Gen. of Militia, Congressman, Governor and Senator. A political sponsor of Calhoun, he was a notable orator. First Officers of McDuffie County, commissioned Feb. 11, 1871, were: A. B. Thrasher, Ord.; J. T. Stovall, Sheriff; R. H. Pearce, Clk. Sup. Ct.; J. D. Montgomery, Tax Rec.; H. W. Young, Tax Col.; John R. Wilson, Sur.; B. E. Pearce, Treas.; R. T. Blanchard, Coroner.

## McINTOSH COUNTY

THIS COUNTY, CREATED DEC. 19, 1793 FROM LIBERTY COUNTY, WAS NAMED FOR the McIntosh family, early settlers, whose name was associated with most events in Georgia history for many years. John McIntosh, with 170 Highlanders, came to Georgia in January 1735 and founded Darien. George N. Ragan was made Tax Collector of McIntosh County Dec. 23, 1793. County officers, commissioned March 25, 1794, were: William Middleton, Sheriff; John Baillie, Clerk of Superior and Inferior Courts; John Richey, Coroner; George N. Ragan, Surveyor. Joseph Clark was commissioned Tax Receiver, Dec. 21, 1794.

## MURRAY COUNTY

MURRAY COUNTY, CREATED BY ACT OF DEC. 3, 1832 FROM CHEROKEE, originally contained Whitfield, Walker, Catoosa, Dade and part of Chattooga Counties. Settled by people from Tenn., N. C., and Ga., it was named for Thomas Walton Murray (1790-1832). A native of Lincoln County, a lawyer, legislator, and speaker of the house, he acquired distinction for his independence and honesty. A candidate for Congress, he died before the election. First officers of Murray County, commissioned March 20, 1833, were: Nelson Dickerson, Clk. Sup. Ct.; John Sloan, Clk. Inf. Ct.; James C. Barnett, Sheriff; Thomas Gann, Surveyor; Adam Gann, Coroner.

## NEWTON COUNTY

THIS COUNTY, CREATED BY ACT OF THE LEGISLATURE DEC. 24, 1821, IS NAMED for Sergeant John Newton, Revolutionary soldier & companion of Sergeant Jasper for whom Jasper County is named. The County Site is named for Gen. Covington. G. C. Adams, County School Commissioner, in 1893 inaugurated the first free transportation for public school pupils in the nation. He later founded the first 4-H Club. Nearby is located the famous Methodist College, Emory at Oxford, charter in 1836, named for Bishop John Emory and now a part of Emory University.

## OGLETHORPE COUNTY

THIS COUNTY CREATED BY AN ACT OF THE LEGISLATURE DEC. 19, 1793, is named for Gen. James E. Oglethorpe, founder of Georgia. Born in London, England, Dec. 22, 1696, Oglethorpe left England in Nov. 1732 with 116 settlers and arrived at Yamacraw in Jan. 1733, where he established the settlement which is now the city of Savannah. He later brought over 150 Scotch Highlanders & some German Protestants from Salzburg. He finally to England in 1743 and resigned his Georgia Charter to the British Government in 1752. Always a friend of America, he died July 1, 1785.

## PAULDING COUNTY

CREATED DECEMBER 3, 1832, AND NAMED FOR JOHN PAULDING, ONE OF THE captors of Major Andre, accomplice of Benedict Arnold. Van Wert, the first county seat, was named for another of the captors. When Polk County was created in 1851, Dallas became the Paulding county seat. Construction of the Seaboard and Southern Railroads through the county, and introduction of the textile industry, were of much importance to county growth. In 1864 major battles were fought at New Hope and Dallas.

## PICKENS COUNTY

CREATED DECEMBER 5, 1853, AND NAMED FOR GENERAL ANDREW PICKENS OF Revolutionary fame. The first settlements sprang up along the Old Federal Road which followed in general the route of the highway through Tate, Jasper and Talking Rock. Mount Oglethorpe (formerly called Grassy Knob), Burrell Top of Burnt Mountain and Sharp Top Mountain dominate the skyline in the northeastern part of the county; to the southwest is Sharp Mountain. Coming of the railroad in 1883 made possible development of a large and important marble industry.

## UPSON COUNTY

THIS COUNTY, CREATED BY ACTS OF THE LEGISLATURE DECEMBER 15 AND 20, 1824, is named for Stephen Upson, a well known lawyer of Lexington, Ga. Lt. Gen. John B. Gordon, famed Confederate leader called "second to the great Lee" was born in Upson County at the settlement of Black Ankle near the Flint (or Thronateeska) River. Among the first County Officers were: Sheriff Martin W. Stamper, Clerk of Superior Court James W. Cooper, Clerk of Inferior Court and Treasurer James P. Portis, Tax Receiver Amos McLendon, Tax Collector Joseph Rodgers, Coroner Shadrach Ellis and Surveyor William Silman

## WALKER COUNTY

CREATED DECEMBER 18, 1833, AND NAMED FOR MAJOR FREEMAN WALKER of Augusta, prominent attorney and United States Senator. Here the fierce Chickamaugas preyed upon pioneers, and were in turn defeated and driven away; here Federals and Confederates locked in combat in 1863.

Lookout Mountain and its spur Pigeon Mountain on the east of the county provide spectacular scenery. Rich coal and iron deposits abound; between the mountains lie fertile valleys.

## WALTON COUNTY

THIS COUNTY, CREATED BY ACTS OF THE LEGISLATURE DECEMBER 15 & 19, 1818, is named for George Walton, signer of the Declaration of Independence. Walton, born in Va. in 1749 came to Savannah when 20 to study law. Elected Secretary of the first Provincial Congress of Ga. in '75 he was also President of the Council of Safety. He served in the Continental Congress from Jan. '76 till Oct. '81. As a Col. of militia he was wounded and captured at the Battle of Savannah. He was Governor in '79 & '80, and again in '89 & '90; U. S. Senator in '95 & '96. He died Feb. 2, 1804.

## WASHINGTON COUNTY

WASHINGTON, GEORGIA'S NINTH COUNTY AND FIRST IN THE NATION TO BE named for George Washington, was created in 1784 for granting land to soldiers for Revolutionary War services.

Court House Square, located on the old stage coach road from Louisville to Milledgeville, is on the Dixie and Nancy Hart Highways.

The present Court House Building, he third, was erected in 1899. The first was burned in "the great fire" March 24, 1855, when only five buildings in the entire town were left. The second, built with a tax levied by the State Legislature, was burned in 1864 by Sherman on his "March to the Sea."

It is claimed that more Confederate soldiers went from Washington county than from any other county in the state. Fifteen military companies were organized here.

## THOMAS COUNTY

THOMAS COUNTY WAS CREATED BY LEGISLATIVE ACTS OF DEC. 23 AND 24, 1825 introduced by Thomas J. Johnson, and named for Gen. Jett Thomas, War of 1812 hero. First settlers included John Parramore, Shadrick Atkinson, E. Blackshear, N. R. Mitchell and John Hill Bryan. The first governing justices were Aaron Everett, Thomas Dekle, Duncan Ray, Simon D. Hadley and A. McMillan. The home of prosperous farms, beautiful mansions, with industry and culture working side by side.

## TIFT COUNTY

THIS COUNTY, CREATED BY ACT OF THE LEGISLATURE AUGUST 17, 1905, is officially named for Nelson Tift, well known businessman, legislator and Mayor of Albany. The organizers also had in mind his nephew Henry Hardin Tift, who founded Tifton in 1872 when he built a saw mill and commissary here though the first postoffice was not established until 1887. Among the first County Officers were: Sheriff J. B. Baker, Ordinary W. S. Walker, Clerk J. E. Peoples, Tax Receiver J. A. Marchant, Tax Collector J. Henry Hutchinson, Treasurer S. F. Overstreet, Coroner J. E. Johns, and Surveyor J. T. Webb.

## TROUP COUNTY

GEORGE MICHAEL TROUP WAS BORN SEPTEMBER 8, 1780 AND DIED APRIL 26, 1856. During Troup's tenure as Governor of Georgia (1823-1827), Troup County was created on December 16, 1826. Boundaries of original Troup County extended from the Flint River on the east to the Chattahoochee River on the west. East and southern boundaries were reduced on December 24, 1827, to its approximate present size. Governor Troup was buried in Montgomery County, Georgia. He was twice married and father of six children.

## TWIGGS COUNTY

TWIGGS COUNTY WAS CREATED BY ACT OF DEC. 14, 1809 FROM Wilkinson County. It was named for Gen. John Twiggs (1750-1816), born in Maryland, resident of Burke County, a leader in the Revolution and against the Indians. He signed treaties with the Creeks at Galphinton in 1785 and at Shoulderbone in 1786. Edmund Nunn was commissioned Sheriff, Dec. 14, 1809, James Patton was made Tax Rec. and James Spann, Tax Col. May 5, 1810. Other County Officers, commissioned May 29, 1810, were: Ewin Hart, Clerk Inf. Court; Peter L. Levingston, Surveyor; James Wheeler, Coroner.

elsewhere on this square. In 1922 a fire destroyed the interior of the present building which was rebuilt in fire resistant materials. Fully refurbished in 1985, the building contains county offices, the Superior Court and virtually complete county records.

## PIERCE COUNTY

THIS COUNTY, CREATED BY ACT OF THE LEGISLATURE DECEMBER 18, 1857, is named for Franklin Pierce, New Hampshire Democrat and fourteenth President of the United States, 1853 to '57. He was a General in the Mexican War. Blackshear, incorporated December 16, 1859, is named for General David Blackshear, noted Georgia Indian fighter. Among the first County Officers were: Sheriff John Donalson, Clerk of Superior and Inferior Courts David Rowell, Ordinary Aaron Dowling, Tax Receiver John Sugg, Tax Collector Edmund Thomas, Coroner James Thomas and Surveyor James E. Blitch.

## POLK COUNTY

CREATED DECEMBER 20, 1851 AND NAMED FOR PRESIDENT JAMES KNOX POLK, Cedartown is fittingly named for the trees which flourish in this beautiful valley. The city is a railroad center, has a thriving textile industry, and a large paper mill. Rockmart, thirteen miles to the east, has textile mills that give the area much employment and a large payroll, and as well is the center of portland cement production.

## PULASKI COUNTY

THIS COUNTY, CREATED BY ACT OF THE LEGISLATURE DECEMBER 13, 1808, IS named for Count Casimir Pulaski, Polish hero of the Revolutionary War who died fighting in Georgia and is buried at Savannah. Court was to be held at the home of Isham Jordan until the County Site was selected at Hartford in 1810. It was moved across the Ocmulgee to Hawkinsville in 1836 when this town was incorporated. Among the first County Officers were: Sheriff Lewis Holland, Clerk of the Superior Court Richard H. Thomas, Clerk of Inferior Court John Rainey, Coroner William Brocken and Surveyor John Bush.

## SEMINOLE COUNTY

THIS COUNTY, CREATED BY ACT OF THE LEGISLATURE JULY 8, 1920, IS NAMED for the Seminole Indians. Members of the Creek Confederacy, the Seminoles (meaning "separatist") left the main body in Georgia and settled in Florida. After two bloody wars in 1817-'18 and 1835-'42, under Osceola, the majority were moved to western reservations but several hundred escaped to the Everglades where the tribe still dwells. Among the first County Officers were: Sheriff J. M. Richardson, Clerk of Superior Court C. L. Reynolds, Ordinary J. H. Goodwin, Tax Collector W. O. Hodges, Treasurer R. T. Bolton, Coroner Jessie E. Yates and Surveyor W. H. Hickson.

## STEWART COUNTY

THIS HANDSOME STRUCTURE WAS BUILT IN 1895 IN THE CLASSICAL STYLE MADE popular by the buildings housing the Columbia Exposition in Chicago (1893-94) to which Lumpkin-born architect John Wellborn Root was a major contributor. It replaced a wooden courthouse built on the same site in 1837. The first seat of county government in 1831 was a small frame structure

Washington County has furnished two Governors – Jared Irwin, 1796 to 1798 and 1806 to 1809, and Thomas W. Hardwick, 1921 to 1923. Gov. Hardwick also had served as United States Senator and Congressman.

## WEBSTER COUNTY

THIS COUNTY, CREATED BY ACT OF THE LEGISLATURE DECEMBER 16, 1853, was originally named Kinchafoonee. It was organized in 1854 at which time Preston was chartered. An Act of February 21, 1856, changed the name to Webster in honor of Daniel Webster, New England orator and statesman. Among the first Kinchafoonee County Officers in 1854 were: Sheriff Carey T. Cox, Clerk of Superior Court James G. Hall, Clerk of Inferior Court John D. King, Ordinary E. B. Swiney, Tax Receiver William McLendon, Tax Collector Lucius Sanders, Surveyor Jno. McCain and Coroner James R. Moore. The first Webster County Officers included: Sheriff John P. Beaty, Clerk of Superior Court James G. M. Ball, Clerk of Inferior Court Wm. R. Redding, Ordinary David G. Rogers, Tax Receiver Eben E. Little, Tax Collector Alexander Winzor, Surveyor John McCain, Coroner John D. Jones and Commissioners George M. Hay, John W. Easters, William H. Hallen, Henry W. Spears and James G. M. Ball.

## WHEELER COUNTY

THIS COUNTY, CREATED BY ACT OF THE LEGISLATURE AUG. 14, 1912, IS NAMED for Gen. Joseph Wheeler, famous Confederate Cavalry leader and Major General of Cavalry in the Spanish War. He twice saved Augusta from Kilpatrick's Union Cavalry, at Waynesboro, Ga., in 1864 and at Aiken, S. C. in '65. For his brilliant work at Santiago Teddy Roosevelt called him "a regular gamecock." First County Officers were: Ordinary Wm. B. Kent, Superior Court Clerk John Durden Brown, Sheriff J. F. Wright, Tax Receiver W. T. Hadden, Tax Collector J. A. Martin, Treasurer Daniel Pope, Surveyor E. Miller and Coroner James J. Brantley.

## WILKES COUNTY

WILKES COUNTY, AN ORIGINAL COUNTY, WAS CREATED BY THE CONSTITUTION of Feb. 5, 1777 from Creek and Cherokee Cessions of June 1, 1773. At first, it contained all of Oglethorpe, Elbert, Lincoln, and parts of Taliaferro, Hart, Warren, and Madison Counties. It was named for John Wilkes (1727-1797), English politician and publicist, who strongly opposed measures leading to war with the colonies. First County Officers were: John Dooly, Sheriff, comm. Feb. 9, 1778; Samuel Creswell, Surveyor, comm. Feb. 18, 1783; Benjamin Catching, Clk. of Sup. and Inf. Cts., comm. Jan. 2, 1785; Howell Jarrett, Coroner, comm. 1790.

Missing County Markers: Baldwin, Chatham, Jefferson, Lumpkin, Muscogee and Whitfield.